The Psychopolitics of Food

The Psychopolitics of Food probes into the contemporary *foodscape*, examining culinary practices and food habits and in particular the ways in which they conflate with neoliberal political economy. It suggests that generic alimentary and culinary practices constitute technologies of the self and the body and argues that the contemporary preoccupation with food takes the form of *rites of passage* that express and mark the transition from a specific stage of neoliberal development to another vis-à-vis a re-configuration of the alimentary and sexual regimes.

Even though these rites of passage are taking place on the borders of cultural bi-polarities, their function, nevertheless, is precisely to define these borders as sites of a neoliberal transitional demand; that is, to produce a cultural bifurcation between 'eating orders' and 'eating dis-orders', by promoting and naturalising certain social logics while simultaneously rendering others as abject and anachronistic.

The book is a worthwhile read for researchers and advanced scholars in the areas of food studies, critical psychology, anthropology and sociology.

Mihalis Mentinis completed this work as part of a postdoctoral research project in the Interdisciplinary Centre for Intercultural and Indigenous Studies (ICIIS), at the Pontifical Catholic University of Chile. He now lives and works in Athens, Greece.

Concepts for Critical Psychology: Disciplinary Boundaries Re-thought

Series editor: Ian Parker

Developments inside psychology that question the history of the discipline and the way it functions in society have led many psychologists to look outside the discipline for new ideas. This series draws on cutting edge critiques from just outside psychology in order to complement and question critical arguments emerging inside. The authors provide new perspectives on subjectivity from disciplinary debates and cultural phenomena adjacent to traditional studies of the individual.

The books in the series are useful for advanced level undergraduate and postgraduate students, researchers and lecturers in psychology and other related disciplines such as cultural studies, geography, literary theory, philosophy, psychotherapy, social work and sociology.

Published Titles:

Surviving Identity
Vulnerability and the psychology of recognition
Kenneth McLaughlin

Psychologisation in Times of Globalisation
Jan De Vos

Social Identity in Question
Construction, subjectivity and critique
Parisa Dashtipour

Cultural Ecstasies
Drugs, gender and the social imaginary
Ilana Mountian

Decolonizing Global Mental Health
The psychiatrization of the majority world
China Mills

Self Research
The intersection of therapy and research
Ian Law

The Therapeutic Turn
How psychology altered Western culture
Ole Jacob Madsen

Race, Gender, and the Activism of Black Feminist Theory
Working with Audre Lorde
Suryia Nayak

Perverse Psychology
The pathologization of sexual violence and transgenderism
Jemma Tosh

Radical Inclusive Education
Disability, teaching and struggles for liberation
Anat Greenstein

Religion and Psychoanalysis in India
Critical clinical practice
Sabah Siddiqui

Ethics and Psychology
Beyond codes of practice
Calum Neill

The Psychopolitics of Food
Culinary rites of passage in the neoliberal age
Mihalis Mentinis

Deleuze and Psychology
Philosophical provocations to psychological practices
Maria Nichterlein and John R. Morss

Rethinking Education in Co-operative Schools
Social justice, discourse and voice
Gail Davidge

'In *The Psychopolitics of Food*, Mihalis Mentinis offers a thoughtful and original analysis of the contemporary foodscape in relation to neoliberalism. From an extension of the critical analysis of the "celebrity chef" to a consideration of the psychopolitical function of placentophagy, the book is well-grounded in food studies scholarship while extending this work in provocative ways. Its global perspective is particularly welcome as it uses Chile and Greece as informative case studies that interrogate the role of food in these countries' neoliberal transformations. And the final chapter provides an insightful engagement with anorexia that shifts away from a psycho-pathological approach to one that reads it as a form of culinary resistance to neoliberalism. Overall, the book's exploration of how culinary rites of passage contribute to neoliberal development is both theoretically rich yet accessible to all readers. It marks an important intervention in the trajectory of food studies scholarship.'

– *Peter Naccarato, Professor of English & World Literatures, Marymount Manhattan College, USA*

'The uniqueness and strength of this thought provoking book is its focus on a very ordinary function in everyday life: eating practices. By focusing on food consumption, Mentinis clearly depicts how neoliberal transformation of our societies does not only affect our lives abstractly somewhere in the "economy" but that it is inextricably intertwined in the restructuring of the very fabric of our daily life practices.'

– *Athanasios Marvakis, Professor in Clinical Social Psychology, Aristotle University of Thessaloniki, Greece*

'A disturbing book that shows that our cooking culture *boom* is committed to the transformation of everyday forms of life into a cannibalistic/anorectic form of exploitation. A front-line exercise of grounded and cunning critique of ideology, opening truly new questions and insights for social theory and research, as well as for the lay understanding that the global path to our future is concretely passing through our own culinary/alimentary/sexual regimes.'

– *Andrés Haye, Associate Professor of Psychology and member of the Interdisciplinary Center for Intercultural and Indigenous Studies, Pontifical Catholic University of Chile, Chile*

The Psychopolitics of Food
Culinary rites of passage in the neoliberal age

Mihalis Mentinis

LONDON AND NEW YORK

First published 2016
by Routledge
2 Park Square, Milton Park, Abingdon, Oxon OX14 4RN

and by Routledge
711 Third Avenue, New York, NY 10017

First issued in paperback 2018

Routledge is an imprint of the Taylor & Francis Group, an informa business

© 2016 Mihalis Mentinis

The right of Mihalis Mentinis to be identified as author of this work has been asserted by him in accordance with sections 77 and 78 of the Copyright, Designs and Patents Act 1988.

All rights reserved. No part of this book may be reprinted or reproduced or utilised in any form or by any electronic, mechanical, or other means, now known or hereafter invented, including photocopying and recording, or in any information storage or retrieval system, without permission in writing from the publishers.

Trademark notice: Product or corporate names may be trademarks or registered trademarks, and are used only for identification and explanation without intent to infringe.

British Library Cataloguing in Publication Data
A catalogue record for this book is available from the British Library

Library of Congress Cataloguing in Publication Data
Names: Mentinis, Mihalis, author.
Title: The psychopolitics of food : culinary rites of passage in the neoliberal age / Mihalis Mentinis.
Description: Abingdon, Oxon; New York, NY : Routledge, 2016. |
Series: Concepts for critical psychology |
Includes bibliographical references and index.
Identifiers: LCCN 2015049228 (print) | LCCN 2016005676 (ebook) |
ISBN 9781138182561 (hardback) | ISBN 9781315646367 (ebook)
Subjects: LCSH: Food habits–Social aspects. | Food habits–Psychological aspects. | Food habits–Political aspects. | Gastronomy–Social aspects. | Neoliberalism–Social aspects.
Classification: LCC GT2850 .M46 2016 (print) |
LCC GT2850 (ebook) | DDC 394.1/2–dc23
LC record available at http://lccn.loc.gov/2015049228

ISBN 13: 978-1-138-54984-5 (pbk)
ISBN 13: 978-1-138-18256-1 (hbk)

Typeset in Sabon
by Out of House Publishing

For Maria S.

Contents

Foreword by Ian Parker   x
Acknowledgements   xii

Introduction: culinary rites of passage in the neoliberal age   1

1 From unemployment to creative adaptability: romanticised chefs and the psychopolitics of gastroporn   9

2 From the semiotic to the symbolic: placentophagy and the name-of-the-chef   28

3 From colonialism to neoliberal multiculturalism: a Mapuche spice in the Chilean national cuisine   41

4 From East to West: economic crisis and the cooking of the new Greeks   60

5 From eating to starving: gastrosexual men and anorectic women   78

Conclusion: towards a theory of anorectic cannibalism   96

Bibliography   103
Index   119

Foreword

The comedian Tommy Cooper once asked the audience if they liked food, and then replied to his own question 'I do, I don't eat anything else'. Which is funny at one moment but also, for psychologists who are versed in the panoply of 'food disorders' in contemporary culture, also poignant, for most likely they will be asking themselves what to do with people who eat things other than food. What is food? This book asks that question in a quite different way from how it is usually addressed in psychological journals and textbooks. The angle from which it asks the question is not defined by psychiatry – that, among other things, is a discourse and practice about food and what we should do with it – but begins with anthropology. Mihalis Mentinis takes the step back from psychology that all critical psychologists must take, and does this to frame the question about our relationship to food from the work of Claude Lévi-Strauss to show us that this relationship marks a 'rite of passage'. This kind of anthropology feeds a series of theories that are served up in the course of the book; structural linguistics in the work of Saussure and then the semiological and 'post-structuralist' descriptions of the transformation of one system of meaning into another that enable reconnection with the political that the discipline of psychology too-often tries to shut out. These theories are weighed up and cooked for us before our very eyes so we are then able to return to how psychologists deal with the question. Instead of psychology, then, 'psychopolitics'.

The book is careful to take its distance from each and every psychologising attempt to incorporate and regurgitate theories that the discipline finds to its taste – including anthropology – and, instead, enables us to assess the claims made by these theories in their own terms, demonstrating that 'psychology' itself is part of the problem, misleading us about the nature of food and its place in culture. So, the notion of 'rite of passage' informs the original theoretical framework which is elaborated through the book. Instead of treating a rite of passage as a simple transition from childhood to adulthood, which is the simplistic and banal way that psychology usually incorporates anthropology, Mentinis argues that collectively shared rites of passage are the sites in which we experience a series of culinary transformations. These transformations are not rooted in pre-history or – to avoid another potent psychological motif – a 'pre-verbal' stage of individual development into which the researchers dig and pretend to find the origins of our thinking. No, these transformations are to be found under capitalism, in the mutations of one phase of neoliberalism into the next. Psychoanalysis in this account is thus rescued from the hands of the psychologists and re-configured to be in its natural home again with anthropology and the human sciences, a theory or set of theories of culture and our-selves and our food within it.

In chapter 10 of Revelation the angel says 'eat the book', and this demand that one should incorporate the word of God and make it flesh is chewed over by the psychoanalyst Jacques Lacan in order that we should arrive at an ethics of sublimation. Sublimation as the work of culture, and of the way we make and consume cultural products like books, is an alternative to repression. Instead of pushing away forms of discourse and other culturally meaningful practices, shutting them out and refusing to think about them, the work of sublimation entails a different kind of engagement and incorporation of signifiers. *The Psychopolitics of Food: Culinary Rites of Passage in the Neoliberal Age* is about the incorporation of what was outside into our insides, and it explores the nature of food as an object that is always necessarily at the border between the two, 'outwith' the body, and of the mind that mainstream psychology tries to make its own preserve.

Ian Parker
University of Leicester

Acknowledgements

Thanks to all those who read and commented on draft chapters, provided me with ideas, information and references, and, in one way or another, contributed to the writing and publication of this book. Many thanks to Dimitris Anagnostou, Svenska Arensburg, Gregory Bistoen, Erica Burman, Rania Erimaki, Ian Parker, Nicolas Valiente, Andreas Vatsinas, Yiannis Vogiatzis and Jan De Vos. Special thanks also to my colleagues in the Interdisciplinary Center for Intercultural and Indigenous Studies (ICISS) at the Pontificia Universidad Católica de Chile: to Andres Haye, Fernanda Kalazich, Juan Loera, Jose Mariman, Bastien Sepúlveda, as well as all the researchers of the 'conflict and subjectivity' line. This book would not have been possible without the help and support of all these people.

Introduction
Culinary rites of passage in the neoliberal age

Elias Canetti writes in *Crowds and Power*, that:

> one tends to see only the thousand tricks of power which are enacted above ground, but these are the least part of it. Underneath, day in, day out, is digestion and again digestion. Something alien is seized, cut up into small bits, incorporated into oneself, and assimilated ... it is clear that all the phases of this process, and not only the external and half-conscious ones, must have their correspondence in the psyche.
>
> (2000, p. 210)

Canetti is right in many respects here, but notwithstanding the discernment of this observation, there is a phase in his alimentary chain which is conspicuous by its absence: 'cooking'. The explosion of food and culinary culture at this historical juncture, forces us to take cooking and eating seriously, and subject both to theoretical scrutiny. Cooking cannot be ignored or merely classified as a neutral and wholly innocent concoction; rather, as with all material culture, it must be examined in relation to broader ideological practices (Cusack, 2000), and deemed to have manifold psychopolitical functions; as having "correspondence in the psyche" as Canetti puts it.

Foucault's (1986) claim that the Greek preoccupation with controlling diet had given way to a modern obsession with sex seems to be no longer entirely true for our contemporary lifeworld. Rather food, albeit often conflated with sex, is today claiming centre-stage as the privileged site of moral restriction, scientific inquiry and individuating reflexivity (see Probyn, 1999; Taylor, 2010). If, as Deleuze and Guattari have argued, within a machinic assemblage "what regulates the obligatory, necessary, or permitted intermingling of bodies is above all an alimentary regime and a sexual regime" (1987, p. 90), and given that the intermingling of bodies is indissolubly connected with the intermingling of selves, then it perhaps goes without saying that contemporary reconfigurations in the 'foodscape' (Potter and Westall, 2013) have a transformative effect on both, bodies and selves. It is in this precise sense that this book claims to be about culinary and alimentary psychopolitics, which is to say that, it is concerned with the ways in which eating and cooking practices are related to the production and configuration of the psyche within a constantly changing neoliberal symbolic and material assemblage. By critically examining this psychopolitical function, the book puts forward the thesis, as an over-arching theoretical and analytical framework, that contemporary culinary culture could be understood as a series of culinary/alimentary rites of passage that mark the transition from one stage of neoliberal development to another.

We know from Lévi-Strauss (1983) that the uniquely human act of cooking, the transformation by fire of the raw material into cooked food, serves as a metaphor for the relationship between nature and culture. The same metaphor seems to be replicated in the rites of passage that in all societies, at least originally, mark a transition from childhood, seen as a state of incompleteness, to adulthood. Most of the time, as Harpur (2009) asserts, these rites of passage are structured around the 'cooking' of the individual; his or her death as a 'natural' being through the symbolic application of fire, heat, smoke, hot water or steam. 'Cooking', an expurgation based on smoke or the incensory, is also employed for such cases when somebody falls back into nature or deeply into biology, and, as a consequence, is in danger of 'rotting' in his or her absolute rawness: "we cook ourselves, then, at moments of biological crisis", argues Harpur, "in order to transform ourselves from natural beings into social beings" (ibid, p. 94). It is my argument, then, that the contemporary preoccupation with food and cooking takes the form of a ritualistic transition of the self and culture from one specific stage of neoliberal development to another vis-à-vis the re-configuration of the alimentary (and sexual) regime.

This is not to say, however, that these rites of passage actually engender neoliberal psychopolitical demands, even though they do contribute to their symbolic articulation and their constitution as social logics. In the same way that a puberty rite of passage does not bring about the biological and psychological maturation of the person, but rather marks the transition to adulthood, culinary rites of passage define transitory, liminal spaces where the relation between the 'immature' past and the 'mature' future is ritualistically re-negotiated and re-invented. To put it in another way, culinary rites of passage are taking place on the borders of cultural bi-polarities (e.g. traditional/modern, feminine/masculine, East/West, etc.) – as such they are neither homogeneous nor complete, but rather asymmetrical, hodgepodge and incomplete – and their function is to define and delineate bifurcations between 'eating orders' and 'eating dis-orders', by promoting and naturalising certain social logics while simultaneously rendering others as abject and anachronistic. In this sense, the present book is driven by what Barthes (1972) in *Mythologies* described as an impatience at the sight of naturalness by which the media dress up what is actually a historical reality, and its principal aim is to demystify today's culinary and alimentary culture as a form of dehistoricised and naturalised *myth* (see also Hebdige, 1979; Brownlie et al., 2005; Smith, 2012).

That culinary rites of passage are even possible at all is down to food's 'anomalousness' (see Lévi-Strauss, 1983). Food is an 'anomalous' category not simply because of its unidirectional transformation from raw to cooked, and thus from nature to culture (see Elyada, n.d.), but mainly because of its bidirectional movement between opposing categories: between the material and immaterial, the human and the sacred, the lower classes and the upper classes, the traditional and the modern, the feminine and the masculine and so on and so forth, with the former pole normally signifying 'nature' and 'biology' or a more 'natural' state of culture, and the latter an 'advanced' state of culture. As Appadurai (1981) points out, food has a semiotic force that remains tacit until it is "animated by particular cultural concepts and mobilized by particular social contexts" (p. 509). It is this tacit semiotic force that allows food and cooking to be claimed by a number of diverse and competing discourses/practices (e.g. aesthetic, medical, national, economic, etc.) (see Warde, 1994), and gives them a 'magical' ritualistic aura.

Inasmuch as food is primarily a material form, it affects the very materiality of our bodies and our intermingling with others. To the extent to which it is a language (see also Barthes, 1972; Lévi-Strauss, 1983) it interpellates us and positions us; tells us what we are and what we are not; commands what we should be (or not be), how we should act (or should not act). The fact that food constitutes a language means that we do not necessarily need to physically consume a given dish or cook it ourselves in order to be exposed to its message and be affected by its symbolics and metaphorics. When watching food being prepared in a TV kitchen, for instance, we are interpellated at least in two crucial respects: first, by the explicit instructive nature of the language employed by the chefs that orders us what to do and not do; second, the mere act and way of transforming some separate raw materials into an edible composition communicates to the audience a psychopolitical aesthetic, a social logic containing forms of personhood, ways of being a body, and forms of relating to others and the world.

TV kitchens are the most privileged sites of culinary rites of passage; the liminal, 'sacred' paces in which psychopolitical demands are communicated and transmitted, and the necessary disjunctions, supersessions, substitutions and re-inventions are symbolically enacted. In a sense, they are border-like places constructed as *heterotopias* (Foucault, 1984), spaces of otherness free of power relations and hierarchical structures. They resemble domestic kitchens (although not exactly), whilst also encapsulating certain aspects of professional kitchens without necessarily being entirely professional either. Being free from responsibilities, forms of human interaction, hierarchical relations, pressure, not to mention the outright mess and clutter of both real domestic and/or professional kitchens, TV kitchens are thus staged as spaces of unrestricted and untrammelled individual creative activity that negotiate the private and the public, family and wider culture, individuals and the economy, and other cultural bi-polarities, contributing thus to the re-configuration of gender and class relations, national identities, and selfhoods (see Goody, 1982; Floyd, 2004; Brownlie and Hewer, 2011).

The present book consists of five main chapters, each exploring both a particular 'cultural border' as structured by alimentary/culinary practices, and a psychopolitical transitional process that takes place at this border.

Chapter outlines

Chapter 1 discusses the rite of passage from unemployment (and poverty) to creative adaptability, exploring the figure of the celebrity chef in terms of the broader social and political consequences of their public alimentary/culinary interventions. In contradistinction to an observed tendency within food related (mainly sociological) literature to discuss chefs in terms of the decline of authority in our societies, the rise of celebrity culture and the possession of cultural (culinary) capital, this chapter highlights the inadequacies of these approaches by pointing out how reducing TV chefs to mere celebrities fails to account for their unique psychopolitical function. The figure of the celebrity chef is another 'anomalous' category standing in the middle of distinct, and often competing worlds. And like other anomalous figures (angels, vampires, etc.) he has a special affinity and proximity to the world that carries the greatest semiotic value.[1] That said, the celebrity chef does not simply negotiate with opposing 'demons' and deal with

Introduction 5

their polarised and competing values and demands (e.g. tradition vs modernisation), rather, he solves the emerging conflicts in favour of the strongest one, whilst affording the weakest limited, controlled and continually re-negotiable rights in the emerging 'eating order'.

For these reasons, the chapter proposes a culturally immanent understanding of the figure of the celebrity chef, by drawing attention to the way in which they are often described and presented in terms borrowed from German romanticism. Such an approach is considered to be more effective for the specific reason that it allows us to link the 'romanticised' chefs with a particular modality of neoliberal psychopolitics.[2] Focusing on acclaimed and renowned examples of public culinary/alimentary interventions, such as Jamie Oliver's *Ministry of Food* and its attempts to tackle obesity amongst the working classes in Rotherham in the UK, and the initiative *chefs contra el hambre* ('chefs against hunger') in Latin America, the chapter probes into the psychopolitics of 'gastroporn', the culturalisation of unemployment and poverty as a social logic, and the 'creative adaptability' promoted as a response/passage to a new order.

Chapter 2 discusses a culinary/alimentary rite of passage from the semiotic to the symbolic by examining the recent phenomenon of placentophagy in Western cultures. Drawing mainly on Julia Kristeva's (1984) distinction between the 'semiotic' and the 'symbolic', the aim of this chapter is to probe into the tension between these two 'territories' in neoliberalism through the reading of two cases reported in the media, in which a chef and a culinary expert cooked and gourmetised a woman's placenta before offering it to guests and consuming it themselves. In the development of its argument, the chapter makes reference to anthropological evidence concerning the (non-eating) ritualistic treatment of the placenta, looks at the social (stabilising) function of these rituals among pre-modern/indigenous cultures, examines anthropophagy/cannibalism as the incorporation of otherness, and explores the meaning of this contemporary anthropophagic consumption of the visceral organ associated with the mother-fetus relationship. Placenta culinary treatment is discussed in relation to the notion of the 'demise of the paternal authority' in Lacanian psychoanalysis, raising the question of whether placentophagy can be considered a ritualistic attempt to re-establish paternal authority, or whether it should be better understood as a structuring function of neoliberalism.

If Chapters 1 and 2 focus on culinary rites of passage in general terms and explore broader tendencies, attend to the cultural specificity of alimentary/culinary psychopolitics examining the cases of Chile and Greece respectively. Neoliberalism does not exist in a pure form operating according to immutable laws. Rather, it is articulated differently according to particular geo-institutional contexts and historically and geographically specific strategies of transformation and ideological articulations, both across and within nation states (Veltmeyer *et al.* 1997; Yates and Bakker, 2013). This contextual 'embeddedness', as Brenner and Theodore (2002, 2005) have called it, is also something that is reflected in alimentary and culinary practices. I use Chile and Greece as case studies, not merely because they are two distinct illustrative examples that allow us to capture the contextual particularities of alimentary/culinary psychopolitics, but also because these two countries are paradigmatic exemplars of neoliberalism in action. On the one hand, Chile is the first country to have undergone a 'shock therapy' of in-depth neoliberal reforms under the military regime of Augusto Pinochet. This entailed more than four decades of deregulation, reducing the role of the state, extensive privatisation, and the promotion of individualism and spirit of competition, which turned the country, according to measures of neoliberal development, into the most advanced economy of the continent, the 'jaguar' of Latin American economies. On the other hand, Greece is the most recent example of a country in deep economic crisis forced to undergo a fully fledged violent neoliberalisation from scratch. Examining the foodscape and the *tastescape* of these two countries allows us to see the ways in which food is mobilised vis-à-vis a country's relation to neoliberalism, and asendemic to a process of transition.

Chapter 3 discusses the case of Chile and what one could call the rite of passage from colonialism to neoliberal multiculturalism. The chapter brings attention to the way the violent repression and marginalisation of the indigenous populations, and the appropriation of their lands, have gradually been replaced (or, more accurately, supplemented) by a logic of accommodation and co-option, especially as far as the Mapuche population is concerned. Methodologically, I follow the aforementioned neoliberal transition by discussing recent developments in the culinary culture of the country and probing into the 'social life' of an indigenous Mapuche condiment, the *merquèn* (a mixture based on smoked red hot chili peppers). The massive popularisation of what was a hitherto unknown indigenous condiment and its incorporation within both quotidian and gourmet national cuisine, define a passage from a divided nation of an exclusionary neoliberalism to a neoliberal multiculturalism that attempts to unites all Chileans under the spirit of entrepreneurship.

Chapter 4 explores the case of Greece in terms of a rite of passage from East to West. Greece is the most recent case of a 'Western'

Introduction 7

country whose economic crisis and near bankruptcy has been attributed by the EU and national elites to its insufficient neoliberalisation, which, in turn, has been attributed to the Eastern components of its culture, politics and national selfhood. Through a particular chain of signification, a veritable host of things, ranging from tradition to the welfare state, are designated as pertaining to the 'maternal' East, and are consequently rendered 'abject' as they are said to produce stagnation, crisis, and impede 'development' and 'progress'. The chapter argues that the culinary and alimentary transformations that have taken place in the country in recent years are consonant with a broader strategy on behalf of the political system and the ruling elites to systematically rid the country of its eastern elements, deepen individualism and strengthen the entrepreneurial spirit; Methodologically, the chapter develops its argument through the reading of a popular Greek movie entitled *Dangerous Cooking* (2010) which, in culinary terms – through the competition between a renowned chef and an ordinary cook for the same woman – presents the process of transition towards Western forms of rationalisation and entrepreneurship as predicated upon the pacification of class struggle and the development of obedient forms of selfhood.

Finally, Chapter 5 explores a peculiar rite of passage, a transition of resistance that is performed by explicitly rejecting food culture. If the passages discussed in the previous chapters are characterised by a transition towards a new symbolic order and the production and promotion of new 'appetites', then the rite of passage discussed here is an anorectic one, which strikes against appetite, refuses food and initiates a line of a flight. The chapter draws on the Foucaultian concept of the *figure*, as elaborated by Todd May (2012), in order to develop the argument that the neoliberal figures of the entrepreneur and the consumer are substantiated (albeit in an anomalous fashion) in the figures of the 'gastrosexual man' and the 'anorectic woman' as two antithetical subject positions within the sexual/alimentary, that is to say a gastrosexual, regime. On one side, the gastrosexual man, as an entrepreneur of the self, constitutes a powerful figure, one who uses his culinary capital for controlling the becoming of woman, and in order to construct the female body as 'edible'. At the other extreme, the anorectic woman appears as an anti-consumer who refuses food (as well as sexuality, maternity, etc.) altogether in an attempt to escape from the gastrosexual condition. Anorexia is discussed not in its commonsensical depiction as a pathology emanating from an over-compliance with certain standards of beauty, but, rather, as a form of resistance. Resisting simplistic idealisations, however, the chapter subsequently argues that what can indeed be initially viewed as an anorectic flight away from the gastrosexuality, eventually comes to an impasse, and the anorectic transformative process soon gets caught in the web of psychological and psychiatric normative discourses. The chapter ends by offering up an example for conceptualising possible ways out of the impasse of anorexia.

The book culminates with a recapitulation of the main themes discussed in previous chapters through an analysis of two installations/performances of the New York based French artist Prune Nourry, and concludes by prefiguring an ethic of 'anorectic cannibalism' as a response to the neoliberal colonisation of life.

Notes

1 Thus, for instance, alongside the binary pair of man/God there is the anomalous category of the angel, or the figure of Christ that links earth with the heavens. Yet another example of an anomalous category is the figure of the vampire that links the living with the dead. Both the angel and the vampire are closer to God and the dead respectively than to humans and living.
2 Given that messianism was an important dimension of romanticism (McCole, 1993), we can detect more than a hint of resistance towards the romanticisation of the celebrity chefs in the way Jamie Oliver was sarcastically labelled a 'messiah' after his *Ministry of Food* in Rotherham, with the author of the blog *Jamie Go Home* cynically commenting: "Thank goodness a missionary came to show us posh ham and asparagus" (quoted in Warin, 2011, p. 36).

1 From unemployment to creative adaptability

Romanticised chefs and the psychopolitics of gastroporn

Beyond the sociology of the culinary expert

The contemporary obsession with culinary culture and, more particularly, the prominence of the now ubiquitous figure of the celebrity chef has been the subject of much critical academic attention, primarily from a perspective that focuses on the emergence and promotion of lifestyle television hosts – in our case TV chefs – as 'experts' who offer guidance and lifestyle suggestions to members of the public, whilst at the same time examining the particular strategies through which this kind of 'expertise' is constructed (e.g. Chaney, 2002; Davies, 2003; Smith, 2010; Tominc, 2014). In a similar fashion, chefs are also of interest as emerging figures of authority which reflect, as Tominc (2014) observes through recourse to Giddens (1990), broader shifts in patterns of authority in Western societies during the transition from modernity to late modernity. Generally speaking, chefs, both as figures of authority and experts, are discussed in terms of their importance for shaping and expressing the tastes, desires and fantasies of the middle classes, alongside acting as gatekeepers to high social status and symbolic ascension through their promotion of the consumption of particular food and food related commodities (e.g. Hollows, 2003; Lang and Heasman, 2004; Ketchum, 2005; De Solier, 2013; Tominc, 2014).

Within a sociological paradigm of work, authority and expertise are invariably understood as central components of what Bourdieu (1984) – a theoretical touchstone in this kind of work – calls 'cultural intermediaries': these are key figures in the media consumption process (e.g. therapists, artists, fashion designers, etc.) who mediate between production and consumers and are actively involved in the symbolic production of value and taste as part of a hedonistic lifestyle (see Binkley, 2006). Cultural intermediaries acquire their status of authority and expertise through the accumulation of what Bourdieu (1984) calls 'cultural capital' (one's skills, training, education, knowledge, etc.). Celebrity chefs, via their role as a specific form of cultural intermediary, are thus said to be in possession of and invest in a particular type of cultural capital which in food related literature is defined as 'culinary capital'. It is the possession of this specific form of culinary capital that forms the basis of their legitimacy as arbiters of culinary taste (see Bell, 2002 cited in Ashley et al., 2004; Naccarato and Lebesco, 2012; De Solier, 2013). Through their role as a cultural intermediary, the celebrity chef is seen as performing a number of functions, some of which are even contradictory; these range from shaping the audience's culinary tastes and disseminating a new consumerist culinary culture, to democratising food knowledge and providing people with the opportunity and means through which to acquire culinary capital themselves (Bell, 2002 cited in Ashley et al., 2004; Tominc, 2014).

Inherent to most approaches within cultural and food studies is an interest in the association of the figure of the celebrity chef with the business sector, with scholars probing into the marketing process by which celebrity chefs become or are consciously created as 'brands', each with their own distinct image and appeal so as to distinguish him/her from their competitors. These 'brand' chefs are subsequently discussed in relation to a variety of industrial concerns, usually related to media interests, the highly competitive restaurant scene and its demand for 'unique' culinary styles and 'signatures', and in terms of celebrity chefs' ability to generate profits through selling various kinds of spinoff merchandise (cookbooks, kitchenware, seasonings, etc.) as expressive of lifestyle consumption (e.g. Ashley et al., 2004; Turner, 2004; Brownlie et al., 2005; Tonner, 2008; Smith, 2010).

Even though this sociological 'paradigm' does capture important elements of the cultural figure in question, as well as showing sensitivity to the ways in which TV cooking programmes and cookbooks reflect, register and mark certain transitional political demands (e.g. Mennell, 1996, Hollows, 2003; Brownlie et al., 2005; Helstosky, 2010; Tominc, 2014), it nevertheless still fails to adequately capture and account for the psychopolitical specificity of the figure of the celebrity chef. Or, phrased otherwise, by discussing the figure of the chef as a subcategory of the broader categories of celebrity and cultural intermediary, the literature thus remains inattentive to its unique function as a shaman-esque figure performing a rite of passage in accordance with neoliberal psychopolitical transitional demands. To a certain extent, the reason for this neglect is the insufficient attention afforded to both the privileged symbolic function of food itself, and its status as a 'magical' element that links the psychological with the social world in a number of linear and hodgepodge ways.

Food's 'anomalousness', its transitory nature which allows it to move between opposing poles, from 'raw' to 'cooked', from 'nature' to 'civilisation' (Strauss, 1983) – or even its character as an intermediary/transitory object (Winnicott, 1953; Farrell, 2000; Sibbett, 2005) – affords it a privileged function within culinary metaphorics. By both working *with* food and *on* food, the figure of the chef appears to negotiate a number of culturally opposing dualistic-archetypes, such as masculinity and femininity, tradition and modernity, repetition and innovation, stability and flexibility, cosmopolitanism and provincialism and so on, vis-à-vis the making and re-making of the self, whilst taking into account culturally embedded neoliberal transitional demands. In fact, the figure of the chef itself is an anomalous figure also: he (as a primarily masculine subject position) appears to stand betwixt and between two distinct worlds (albeit with a special affinity towards one of the two sides), channelling their spirits and negotiating solutions. Just like other anomalous figures residing on the borders of distinct worlds – e.g. the angels (between heaven and earth) or the vampires (between the dead and the living) (see Elyada, n.d.) – the figure of the chef speaks to our very 'souls', promising us access to a 'higher' level of existence as long as we commit to following his instructions and perform the requisite rite of passage.

For the remaining duration of this chapter I will attempt to produce a critical psychological account of the figure of the celebrity chef, paying particular attention to the way it deals with neoliberal demands, that is, its psychopolitical function. I will set out the terms of my argument by discussing first what can be called the romanticisation of the figure of the chef, and exploring, through recourse to Lacanian psychoanalytic theory, the function of the signifier 'chef' in the neoliberal symbolic order. I then proceed by probing further into the metaphorics of cooking, in particular the conjunction between cooking and the production of the self, before concluding by delineating the aesthetic politics of gastroporn as a form of governmentality. In contradistinction to a commonly observed tendency in food related literature to focus on the relation between food culture and the middle classes, my aim here is to construct an account of the way today's cooking culture registers, marks and promotes forms of creative adaptability to the constantly shifting neoliberal landscape.

The romanticisation of the figure of the chef

The relation between romanticism, food and chefs is neither recent nor a simple one. The Romantic late eighteenth and early nineteenth centuries saw the invention of the restaurant, the sophistication of gastronomy and the emergence of culinary public figures, i.e. the first celebrity chefs (Gigante, 2007). In order to gain prestige and be seen as important personages and artists in their own right, famed culinarians of that period would style themselves as great men of letters, as Romantic geniuses, a pretension that would often make them the butt of satire (Garval, 2007). Even though a detailed account of Romantic ideas is beyond the scope of this chapter, it is important to outline their basic philosophy regarding taste and food, which was developed against Kant's theses. In his *Critique of Judgment* Kant (1987), following in a long philosophical tradition that prioritised seeing and hearing over taste and smell, rejects food and drink as objects of contemplative critical appreciation. Kant's argument holds that taste cannot offer a reflective aesthetic experience; that is to say, no object of gustatory experience can be beautiful due to its hedonic immediacy (as opposed to a disinterested attitude required for the appreciation of the beautiful), the reflexive agreeable or disagreeable sensory response (as opposed to the contemplative activity of one's imaginative engagement with the object) and the subjective relativity of taste (as opposed to the universal assent for something to be beautiful).

Given the subordinate status assigned to taste and appetite by Kantian aesthetic theory, then, Romantics' revision of taste as *gusto* was an attempt to tear down the eminence of sight at the top of the hierarchy of the senses (Gigante, 2007), and writers of food and eating merged gastronomy and philosophy in an attempt to elevate cookery to the level of the fine arts, explicitly referring to the 'art of cookery'. Even though such an endeavour found no reciprocation in conventional philosophy (Korsmeyer, 2007), we can nevertheless trace in it the beginning of the introduction of a complex aesthetics in the configuration of the alimentary regime; an aesthetic dimension which is now indispensable to the alimentary regime and the workings of what I call here culinary metaphorics.[1] Shifts which took place in the culinary culture in the late 1960s and 1970s, particularly within the *nouvelle cuisine* in France, constitute another nodal point in both the development of aesthetics in relation to food and the consolidation of an image of the chef as a culinary artist with his own style and 'signature'. This time, however, aside from his culinary artistic virtuosity, the figure of the chef emerges also as an owner of his own restaurant(s), or at

From unemployment to creative adaptability 13

least as one who desires to escape the condition of working for others, aspiring to become an entrepreneur himself (Gillespie, 1994; Mennell, 1996; Parkhurst Ferguson and Zukin, 1998).

This conjunction in the figure of the chef of two distinct figures, that of the artist and the entrepreneur, has now been consolidated, and constitutes the kernel of the psychopolitical function of the chef. On the one hand, contemporary celebrity chefs have managed to achieve, to an unprecedented extent thus far, a status as culinary artists discursively structured around the Romantic notion of the 'creative genius' and its many iterations ('culinary revolutionary', 'culinary visionary', etc.). Indissolubly connected with this romanticisation is the contemporary aestheticisation of food and the tendency of food scholars with an explicit interest in romanticism to reclaim taste's place among the 'higher' senses, in turn, allowing for food to be the object of gustatory aesthetic appreciation (e.g. Monroe, 2007; Sweeney, 2007, 2012; Brady, 2012; Korsmeyer, 2012). If the German Romantic philosophers and writers of the end of the late eighteenth and early nineteenth century came to replace the priest with the genius artist in their mythology, and the aesthetic experience condensed in the original work of art became a mystical experience and form of knowledge of the world (Kearney, 2005; Peroulis, 2012), then we could say that our epoch has chosen to replace the artist with the chef, or more precisely the culinary artist, and the aesthetic experience condensed in food becomes the experience of the neoliberal order of things. If, as Rauning *et al.* (2001) argue, in the tradition of the aesthetics of the genius and charismatic imagination the truly creative social actors, the designated elect who generate innovations, are marked apart for symbolic ascension, then the figure of the chef, situated within the same tradition and largely described with terms borrowed from German romanticism, also comes to perform pivotal symbolic functions. It is now the chef above all, as a culinary artist, who can capture with his creative imagination the spirit of our neoliberal world, and convey it to the people through food (culinary art). Furthermore, the signifier 'chef' itself also performs a symbolic function which imposes certain alimentary laws, as well as performing the imaginary function of constituting an ideal image of the self to be desired.

At the same time, chefs are also romanticised qua their 'subversive' entrepreneurial activity and success: "what Steve Jobs, Richard Branson and Jamie Oliver have in common [is that] they're all genius innovators, doing things differently, looking beyond how things have always been, to find new ways forward", writes the global director of a coaching agency, before she goes on to provide the exact coordinates of entrepreneurial genius: "come out of the traditional box", work with "intuitive senses" and allow ideas to "stream in from the air around us" (Green, 2014, n.p.). What is romanticised here is a 'psychology' (of the entrepreneurial subject) which promotes adaptability to changing conditions and constant change as its modus operandi: "the entrepreneur always searches for change, responds to it, and exploits it as an opportunity" as Dardot and Naval put it (2013, p. 119).[2] Unlike other entrepreneurial figures, however, the chef does not simply run a successful business (restaurants, food brands, etc.) nor merely engages in creative thinking and the releasing of innovations. In addition to all of this, he is the absolute expert in the actual main product he is involved with, that is food, and he is actively involved (at least in the initial stages) in the actual process of its production as a manual worker. Thus, whilst Steve Jobs cannot produce an 'i'-product by himself, Jamie Oliver can design all of his own dishes by hand – using his own branded ingredients, before serving the final product in the restaurants he owns. The figure of the chef merges and blends entrepreneurial spirit, artistic virtuosity and manual work in the single process of producing one's own distinct product; a product bearing one's unique signature. What the romanticisation of the figure of the chef thus serves to demonstrate, is that capitalism in its most advanced (creative/entrepreneurial) forms does not alienate the worker but, in fact, unites him/her organically with his/her product of work; the self and his/her work become one.

Deleuze and Guattari (1987) assert that within a machinic assemblage "what regulates the obligatory, necessary, or permitted intermingling of bodies is above all an alimentary regime and a sexual regime" (p. 90). This is an important point for our argument concerning the centrality of the figure of the chef within the neoliberal symbolic order. Given that the intermingling of bodies is indissolubly connected to the intermingling of selves, it goes without saying that the chef, as the key figure within the contemporary alimentary regime, has a pivotal psychopolitical function to play. This becomes even more apparent if one considers how Foucault's (1986) claim, that the classical world's preoccupation with controlling diet had given way to a modern obsession with sex, now no longer appears to be valid. Indeed, it appears today that food, and thus the alimentary regime, claims a privileged status as a site of moral restrictions, scientific inquiry and individuating reflexivity (see Probyn, 1999; Taylor, 2010), and therefore plays an even greater role than before in the configuration of the neoliberal assemblage. In other words, what we eat, how and how much we eat, whom we eat with and where we eat are now more important coordinates (or at least equal to) of who we are than our sexual activity.

My wager in this chapter is that we should approach the function of the figure of the chef as operating analogously to Lacan's (1993) 'Name-of-the-Father'. If the Name-of-the-Father is a function associated primarily with the sexual regime, that is to say, a function that ultimately regulates desire and the sexual mingling of bodies, then can we not identify the name 'chef' as corresponding to the aforementioned privileged place of the alimentary regime, and which allows for the engagement with the symbolic in alimentary/culinary terms?[3] The 'name-of-the-chef' imposes an alimentary/culinary law that facilitates a transition towards creative adaptability, by forcing the person to break from its dependency and attachment to the maternal (the family, the 'nanny state', tradition, habit, etc.) and engage with the wider neoliberal symbolic order through a culinary metaphorics of the self. "I set up Fifteen", argues Jamie Oliver on his website, "because I believe young people have untapped talents, often hidden by problems in their home lives (2014, n.p.). The function of the chef so it would seem is to tap talent: "my intention was really simple ... to use the magic of cooking to give young people ... the opportunity to unlock their true talent through great training and mentoring" (Oliver, 2015, n.p.). Cooking is not simply about learning skills and rules, then; rather, it is about 'unlocking' hidden 'true' qualities of the self, and it is predicated upon attaining distance from a state of 'pathological' attachment and dependency, the family in this instance, and negotiating participation to the world of 'opportunity' through the intervention and mentorship of the chef. The 'magic' of cooking, in other words, intersects with discourses on the 'discovery of the true self' and 'self actualisation'; it is about 'cooking' of the self so as to bring out its tastes and flavours.

Cooking the self

Whereas the emphasis on the sexual regime makes desire and sexual conduct that which ultimately need to be primarily controlled and demarcated, with the emphasis gradually shifting towards the alimentary regime it is eating and cooking that now become significant practices of selfhood that need to be shaped and given direction. This is evident in the way cooking is discursively constructed as a magical act of transforming the self: "using the magic of food to transform lives" as the motto in Jamie Oliver's opening page of his *Fifteen* project puts it (Oliver, 2015). More explicitly still, the culinary expert Michael Pollan constructs the relationship between the transformation of the self and cooking by evoking shamanistic imagery of mastering nature's powers:

> I apprenticed myself to masters of fire (barbecue); water (home cooking in pots); air (bread baking); and then earth (fermentation). [I wanted] to explore how each of these amazing technologies of transformation worked on the raw material, but also on us, for in cooking the cook is transformed too.
>
> (quoted in Steel, 2014, n.p.)

To cook is thus to be able to re-configure the self, to perform a transition from a certain type of selfhood to another by mastering the logic of the 'forces' that govern change. The kitchen is not simply the place where survival and pleasure are planned, but in actuality a place to produce the self. As the Italian historian Massimo Montanari writes: "to observe the process of cooking, the transformation of raw materials … the incontrovertible rules of suitability, the order and sequence of actions, can allow to contemplate our relationship with ourselves" (2009, pp. ix–x). This is precisely a metaphorics of cooking indissolubly connected to the production of the self.

If the romanticised name 'chef' thus comes to stand for a function that imposes certain laws that facilitate transitions in culinary/alimentary terms, then the romanticised image of the figure of the chef constitutes a kind of ideal-ego to desire and strive for. The centrality of the alimentary/culinary regime in relation to the organisation of bodies and 'selves' means that metaphors of 'eating', 'incorporation' and 'digestion' (e.g. something is 'eating' somebody, one 'eats' his/her heart out, books can be cooked and so on) become re-signified and claim back something from their old literal character. Thus, to know how to 'cook' well, to be a 'chef', emerges as the most important property of the subject, an organising faculty: a 'chefhood'.

We can understand this imaginary function further as a re-enactment of the Lacanian 'mirror stage' within the symbolic. According to Lacan (2006), during the mirror stage of development, the infant, whose reality is a fragmented one due to insufficient control it has over its motor activity and bodily functions, becomes aware of its mirror image as a unity, albeit an external one. The infant identifies with the alienating image, thus developing an ego and an anticipation of mastery over one's body. The ego, as Homer (2005) argues vis-à-vis Lacan, is formed on an illusory image of wholeness and mastery, and functions to maintain this illusion. In other words, the ego derives from a *mis-recognition* and its dominant characteristic is one of denial, in terms of refusing to accept the reality of fragmentation and alienation. Getting back to our discussion, we know that the contemporary subject is largely a fragmented subject in a twofold manner. First, on a cognitive level, the subject is aware of diverse and conflicting bits of information and opinions among which it can switch rapidly without being able to integrate them into a meaningful whole (Jameson, 1991). Second, and perhaps most pertinently, it is required to occupy several and contradictory subject positions, demonstrating great, but albeit exhausting, flexibility as it moves from subject position to subject position, from job to job, from training to training, and so on (see Jameson, 1991; Parker, 2003). The image of the chef thus constitutes an illusion of 'ideal unity'; a unity, moreover, that brings together 'creativity', 'virtuosity', 'self-actualisation' and 'entrepreneurial spirit'.

Furthermore, the image of the chef is indispensable from the actual activity that symbolises and enacts this unity: cooking. The process of preparing a dish as shown in cooking programmes; a process which entails choosing, preparing and combining unrelated ingredients and composing them into an aesthetic visual and gustatory whole, can thus be said to stand as a metaphor for the coordination of the various fragments of the subject into a functional and aesthetic whole. Cooking programmes are not about teaching people how to cook per se; rather, they are about learning how to develop a faculty of coordination, as well as internalising a logic of adaptability predicated upon the constant configuring and re-configuring of the self according to changing demands and shifting moods of the market: "genius innovators are always willing to *reinvent themselves* and their businesses" says the coaching agency director we met earlier (Green, 2014, n.p., italics added). Simply put, it is all about becoming an 'entrepreneur of oneself' (Foucault, 2008).

Jamie Oliver's *Ministry of Food* intervention in Rotherham is exemplary in this respect of how easily one can slide from a putative mission to improve dieting to a metaphorics of cooking as the (re)configuring of the self. Oliver's interest in the South Yorkshire industrial town of Rotherham, one of the UK's most deprived areas, derives from the fact that the programme itself constructs it as an obesogenic environment, with the intervention's putative aim being to improve people's diets. The *Ministry of Food* is unquestionably about the politics of health and class, promoting self-monitoring, personal responsibility and empowerment as personal qualities which intersect with neoliberal principles of public health (Warin, 2011). There is, however, another dimension to the programme, an implicit semantic structure that goes beyond particular issues and concerns the production of the self as a whole. This implicit semantic structure manifests itself and can be grasped at those moments that the programme fails to be faithful to its stated objective, that is, to its anti-obesity mission. As Hollows and Jones point out, in Oliver's *Ministry of Food* there is a "slippage between a campaign teaching people to eat healthily and one teaching them culinary skills, as if good cooking automatically produced leaner citizens" (2010, p. 310). More interestingly yet still, as these authors go on to argue, is the fact that many of the recipes shown in the programme require the use of relatively expensive materials which, while adding some relative flavour to the food, actually contribute nothing to its nutritional value and dieting qualities. This slippage then, this unbridgeable contradiction, points to a function of cooking that supersedes the need for a healthy diet. In order to really tackle obesity, it would seem, one needs a regimen of a different type than the one facilitated by Oliver's flashy recipes.

If we wish to put it in sloganish terms we could say that the *Ministry of Food* is characterised by a slippage from 'you are what you eat' to the more performative 'you are the way you cook'. The chef functions as someone who can help people break free from dependency and attachment to habit – metonymically appearing as obesity and unemployment – and transition to the world of employment and health. These kinds of programmes culturalise poverty and unemployment, explaining it away as a lack of (culinary) skills, and enticing viewers with both covert and overt fantasies of employment and success as being predicated upon a successful transformation of the self. In other words, they are less about how to cook and more about how to live like a chef (Naccarato and Lebesco, 2012), that is to say, to be like a 'chef'. Hollows and Jones (2010) point out the way in which *Jamie's Ministry of Food* strategies "work to establish particular ways of looking in which the audience is invited to identify with Jamie, that is the ideal image, and distance itself from the show's participants" (p. 313).

In the programme, the representative individual who committed to the transformative rite of passage from unemployment and dependency to creative adaptation was single mum Natasha Whiteman. As Hollows and Jones argue:

> by *improving her cooking* and eating habits under Jamie's tutelage, she is shown not only to achieve a potentially more healthy life for herself and her family, but also to improve 'the self' and achieve social mobility ... [B]y the end of the series, her education in *middle class culinary capital* acts as a qualification to enter catering college and move away from welfare benefits.
>
> (2010, p. 315, italics added)

Moving beyond the purely individual level in order to examine Oliver's programme on a broader scale, we can still identify the symbolic function of the name 'Oliver' and the imaginary function performed by his image. The chef imposes the alimentary and culinary laws which allow the entirety of Britain to break free from habit and dependency – towards the 'nanny state', for example – and move on. Furthermore, Oliver and his cooking activity functions as an imaginary fantasy image of wholeness in whose reflection a fragmented Britain can anticipate a future national unity. It is interesting in this regard that the *Ministry of Food* resonated with hegemonic media circulated discourses and political rhetoric centred on Britain as a 'broken society'. Conceptualised mainly in terms of 'fecklessness', 'culture of disrespect', 'binge drinking', 'crime', 'obesity' and so on, the broken society rhetoric appears metonymically in various instances in the *Ministry of Food* in various ways (Hollows and Jones, 2010).

Oliver, who is notorious for reproducing several variations of the 'fecklessness' discourse in relation to Britain's poor, is a 'fixing' function aiming to put back together the pieces of this so-called broken society. When he laments that "seven times out of ten, the poorest families in this country choose the most expensive way to hydrate and feed their families, the ready meals, the convenience foods" (quoted in Goldhill, 2013, n.p.), does he not, implicitly or otherwise, demand that the poor commit to a metaphoric 'cooking' and engage in the magic of self-transformation? Operating as a televised form of governmentality (Warin, 2011), Oliver's programmes thus undercut their purported health and obesity intervention, conveying instead a neoliberal demand for the overall transformation of the poor, their domestication and re-integration within the nation along more neoliberal lines (Foucault, 1993, Rose, 1996). Consequently, what lurks behind this type of culinary psychopolitics is the justification of unemployment through its conceptualisation as the result of individual lack of volition and effort – while covering over structural factors – together with the promotion of a hard-work ethic, and the concomitant demand for workers' submissiveness and obedience. Oliver is unequivocal in his disapproval of the British youth for being "wet behind the ears", succinctly explaining his rationale as thus:

> When you're unleashing students into an economy where there's trouble with jobs, the ones who haven't got academic verve, they need to have a basic approach to physical work. You need to be able to knock out seven 18-hour days in a row. You need to know what real fucking work is.
>
> (quoted in Tucker, 2011, n.p.)

His mocking of the "mummies" of his younger employees phoning up and complaining to him about their kids working too hard and being too tired (Tucker, 2011) is indicative of the symbolic function of the chef, and how the passage to the aforementioned neoliberal hard-work ethic is predicated upon a breaking from the security and protection of the maternal, both in literal and metaphorical terms. It is a theme appearing invariably and in various forms in Oliver's programmes.

The aesthetic psychopolitics of gastroporn

The term 'gastroporn' has been widely employed in order to designate a number of interrelated aspects of visual culinary culture: the staged sensuality of celebrity chefs, the glamorous images of ingredients and dishes in TV and magazines, which parallel those of pornography, the presentation of the reader and viewer with simulated pleasure, that is, aestheticised images of unattainable gratification that replace actual food (Smart, 1994; Bywater, 2001; Iannolo, 2007; Iggers, 2007). Some commentators discuss gastroporn in terms of what they describe as the contemporary paradox of people spending hours watching cooking shows on the TV, whilst spending very little time actually cooking (Fort, 1999 cited in Ashley et al., 2004; Pollan, 2014 cited in Steel, 2014). For the purposes of the current chapter the term is employed mainly in order to express the fantasy involved in both watching cooking shows and flicking through cookbooks, notwithstanding the unattainable character of the object of pleasure. Moreover, I seek to capture the way gastropornographic interventions do not actually stand for what they claim to stand for, that is to teach people how to cook; but, rather, constitute visual performances that promote and propagate a broader psychopolitical aesthetic which, in turn, attempts to naturalise neoliberal realities.[4]

If the production of a unifying, coordinating faculty, a neoliberal ego, is indissolubly connected to a culinary metaphorics, then the aesthetics of this metaphorics forces us to consider how this ego is largely understood as an artist engaging in an artistic activity which primarily concerns the making and re-making of the self as a work of art, as an aestheticised piece of work. The entrepreneur of oneself (Foucault, 2008) is thus, at the same time, the artist of oneself. Featherstone (1991a) discusses this "aestheticisation of everyday life" in terms of the effacement of the boundary between art and everyday life, and the turning of life itself into a work of art. There is a desire to enlarge oneself, or to realise the self in many forms and feel many sensations, to tranform the body, behaviour and feelings into aesthetic endeavours. Within this framework, some scholars argue that cooking has ceased to be an act performed by a caring self who demonstrates affection for others, replaced by an ethos of self-care which concerns a 'performing self' who manages its workings and takes special care of the aesthetics of its self-presentation (e.g. Probyn, 1999; Ashley *et al.*, 2004). In contradistinction to such discussions as Featherstone's (1991b), however, who links an aesthetics of the self with the emerging middle classes and their attempt to distinguish themselves from the popular classes, my aim is to show how the aesthetic psychopolitics of gastroporn is concerned with the disciplining of the working class, the unemployed and the poor.

Neoliberalism relies on the figure of the artist in order to cover over exploitation, and brand itself as a regime of personal 'freedom' and 'independence', since considering of oneself as an artist creates and enhances the fantasy of an organic connection with one's product of ('artistic') activity, that is also the self, in turn, producing a sense of self-determination. The discursive affinity between a conception of the self as an artist and the psychopolitical demands for creative adaptation is commonly found in periods of economic 'crisis', when transitional imperatives become prominent and of an urgent character (see Mentinis, 2013).[5] Within a system of flexible accumulation characterised by the disappearance of the dividing line between work and leisure, and the rapid shifts between periods of employment and unemployment (Lazzarato, 2011), the figure of the precarious worker, henceforth normalised and moved to the centre of society, is increasingly formulated for a range of occupations according to the template of the generic figure of the 'artist', and structured around bourgeois notions of freedom, flexibility, creativity and risk-taking.

Lorey (2011) describes this artistic paradigm of the self as leading to 'self-precarisation', and as being marked by the refusal of certain sectors of the working class (fee-paying jobs, project activities, etc.) to maintain a stable job and a salary. If we think of middle class status as one maintained by a self-directed relationship to production, and the working class in terms of selling one's labour power as a commodity to others, following directions, having no control over the product of one's work and being more disposable (see Davis, 2013), then thinking of oneself as an artist provides the fantasy that one has escaped working class conditions. By seeking to distinguish themselves from working classes by thinking of themselves as artists, Lorey (2011) argues that these self-precarised workers are, in actual fact, so exploitable that neoliberalism promotes them as role models for new modes of living and working.

The argument I put forward here is that the romanticisation of chefs and the promotion of a culinary culture allow the model of the culinary artist to become hegemonic, the model through which to think the self across the entire social world. Within the culinary metaphorics of selfhood, a culinary artist attempts, much like a Romantic artist, to overcome the differences, contradictions and disharmonies of everyday life and achieve not simply an aforesaid sense of unity, but rather a sense of aesthetic wholeness and completion. Working class viewers in particular are encouraged to forget their actual material conditions and instead think of themselves as autonomous, self-determined entrepreneurs (of the self) and creative agents with their own unique cooking 'signature'. Cooking is the kind of romanticised activity that allows potentially anybody to think of themselves as an artist and 'empower' him/herself through their activity in the kitchen. What we see here is a situation whereby Beuys's dictum "everyone is an artist" achieves its full ideological force. The subject thus emerges as the site of an aestheticised, but ultimately illusory reconciliation of conflicting demands, which remain frustratingly conflictual in the social world (Jay, 1992). When one comes to imagine oneself as both a unique artist and as the actual product of this artistic activity, political organisation henceforth becomes almost impossible. Creative adaptation stands precisely for the abandonment of the belief in collective action and class struggle, and the embracement of a personal aesthetic project.

The campaign *Chefs Contra el Hambre* ('Chefs Against Hunger') is part of the initiative 'Latin America and Caribbean without Hunger', a joint effort on the behalf of several Latin American governments and the Food and Agriculture Organization (FAO) of the United Nations. The project, which counts on the participation of internationally renowned and prestigious chefs and food critics, was initiated in 2008, and its purported mission as set out in the introduction of the published cookbooks is to eradicate hunger in the respective countries by the year 2025, along with an expressed commitment on the part of the participating chefs to improve the lives of the most vulnerable (see: FAO, 2011). Again, as in the case of Oliver's *Ministry of Food* discussed earlier, contradictions emerge at various points between the stated mission to tackle hunger and what this initiative actually does in practice. One notable contradiction in the anti-poverty rhetoric concerns the fact that the most vulnerable members of the population, to whom the cookbooks are supposedly addressed and dedicated to, are highly unlikely to be able to afford them and therefore have access to them. Whilst one can definitely expect a kind of diffusion of the culinary aesthetics appearing in these cookbooks to the wider population, again one must ask: is having access to more recipes in any way related to eradicating hunger? Given that hunger cannot be eradicated with aestheticised photographs of dishes, and given the structural causes of poverty in these respective countries, can we not again detect a certain culturalisation of poverty and hunger running through this gastropornographic initiative? Indeed, the initiative seems to fit better within a psychopolitical culinary metaphorics of selfhood. As the Chilean chef Guillermo Rodríguez, who participates in the initiative, admits: "these kind of initiatives allow making communities realise that they can make new recipes with the ingredients they have always used" (quoted in Via Restó, 2008, n.p.).[6] Or, phrased otherwise, the initiative is not about eradicating hunger but about communities learning how to reinvent tradition and their selves breaking from habit and repetition.

Upon introducing one of the campaign's volumes entitled *Productos del Mar* ('Products of the Sea') co-funded by the Chilean government, the ex-first lady of the country, Celia Morel de Piñera, remained absolutely silent about poverty, unemployment and hunger, focusing instead on the importance of healthy eating for physical and psychological well-being, and placing special emphasis upon the significance of cooking for leading a happy family life. Morel de Piñera concludes her preface by imploring the readers to "read the following pages, learn, cook, and enjoy with the family" (FAO, 2011, p. 7). It is important to note that the slippage here from eradicating hunger to living a healthy life within the family does not actually bypass altogether the problem of hunger. On the contrary, in her preface, Chile's ex-first lady points explicitly to the family's function as a net of social support for its members. In the highly neoliberalised Chile where collective provision and social solidarity is provided through private purchasing of insurance schemes and health care, the family has been rendered particularly responsible for social risks (unemployment, poverty, health, etc.). 'Learning' how to 'cook in the family', therefore, marks a radical transition from dependency on the welfare state to the 'creative freedom' of the family, with individuals encouraged to strive to maximise their own quality of life and happiness as well as that of their families (Rose, 1992). Cooking becomes the primary way through which to transition from 'proletarians of the world unite' to 'proletarians of the world enjoy' (with your families in the kitchen).

Similarly, the *Recetario Internacional del Quinua* ('International Cookbook of Quinoa') cosponsored by the Bolivian government, points to a kind of 'creative' adaptability, with its subtitle: *tradición y vanguardia* ('tradition and pioneering') designating a transitional space of liminality, a betwixt and between where adaptation is negotiated.

Introducing the volume on quinoa, the Bolivian president Evo Morales is the only one to explicitly link local knowledge concerning the cultivation and preparation of quinoa to the survival of the poor: "I personally", writes Morales, "am an example of how quinoa can beat poverty and make us strong" (FAO, 2014, p. xii). But if this is so, the question that emerges once again is whether this cookbook, in fact, has any relevance to the eradication of hunger. Do the poor need more recipes?

Behind the hunger beating rhetoric seems to lurk a politics of quinoa production that bears little connection to the putative mission of the quinoa cookbook. With the discovery of quinoa as a gluten-free high protein superfood and the subsequent explosion of the quinoa market, many indigenous farmers turned to monoculture abandoning the cultivation of diverse crops that provided their communities with a variety of food containing nutritional value. Furthermore, the boom in quinoa prices actually put quinoa out of their reach, with farmers opting to sell quinoa to cover other needs and, instead, buy cheaper, lower in nutritional value food like pasta and rice. This resulted in many quinoa growing areas of Bolivia becoming the most malnourished in the country because farmers could no longer afford to eat their own crops (Richardson, 2014). In other words, the gastropornography of the quinoa cookbook and its pseudo-anti-hunger rhetoric ignore completely the way the poor indigenous population of Bolivia is actually deprived from enjoying the benefits of this plant.

Introducing the quinoa cookbook, the general director of FAO, José Graziano da Silva, explains that quinoa is characterised by "the extraordinary capacity to adapt to different types of agric-ecological floors … to be cultivated in zones with various degrees of humidity, on high and low lands, withstanding high and low temperatures" (FAO, 2014, p. x). This language of strength and adaptability to a wide range of extreme conditions, apart from bearing an affinity to the neoliberal discourse of productive entrepreneurship, autonomy and resilience (Rose, 1992), relates also to the indigenous self. Let us not forget that in the indigenous psychologies of Latin America there is an alimentary metaphorics of the self that brings together food consumption and the constitution of the self/body, something reflected in various indigenous groups naming or nicknaming themselves after their basic staple food (e.g. the indigenous of Mesoamerican calling themselves 'the men of corn'). Praising the qualities of quinoa and teaching new recipes to the Bolivian *campesinos*, then, is not about tackling poverty and hunger. Rather, it is all about the strengthening of an alimentary metaphorics, an identification with quinoa that allows its properties of adaptability and stamina to hardship to suffuse with the quinoa producers and become properties of the self.

The return of the cannibal (part one)

In what was an early gastropornographic endeavour, the Italian Futurists of the opening decades of the twentieth century assigned to food a pivotal role in their project to first disorient and then reorganise Italian culture. The destruction and renewal of alimentary and cooking habits was seen as an intrinsic part of the renewal of Italy as a whole, and in place of pasta that was said to be draining the Italians of their energy, creativity and intelligence, Futurists proposed food sculptures or odd food pairings such as meat and cologne (Helstosky, 2010). The radical transformation of what was thought to be a backward Italian self was anticipated and actually promoted through an extreme aestheticisation of food, which, in turn, anticipated a certain fascist politics. Filippo Marinetti's (1932) *La cucina futurista*, which consciously broke with Italian culinary tradition, contains an interesting scene called the 'dinner of white desire'. At the dinner, a group of Africans feast on aestheticised white food in order to exorcise their erotic desire and their yearning to conquer Europe: "a soup of cold milk with chunks of mozzarella and white grapes", a "tray laden with pieces of coconut studded with nougat, enclosed in layers of butter and arranged on a bed of boiled rice and whipped cream" (quoted in Helstosky, 2010, p. 132). The aestheticisation of white food and whiteness, as such, reflected Futurists' impatience with Mussolini's Fascist regime for not commanding a greater empire sooner. As Helstosky (2010) notes, food became an urgent and visceral means through which to compel the Fascist regime to act.

The aestheticisation of politics within the discourse of fascism identified by Benjamin (2005), in the case of Italy was preceded by an aestheticisation of food by the Italian Futurists. The consumption of 'white' aestheticised food in Marinetti's banquette represented what was understood as a violation of the alimentary and sexual regimes that defined the distance, or type of contact permitted among the racialised white and black bodies. The aestheticisation of 'white' food as the object of the blacks' desire formed the basis of the aestheticisation of the means employed in order to prevent its 'conquest', and thus the violation of a certain alimentary and sexual regime. In this sense, when Mussolini's foreign minister, Galeazzo Ciano, compared the bombs exploding upon fleeing Ethiopians in 1936 to "flowers bursting into bloom" (quoted in Jay, 1992, p. 44) he was bringing to its completion the Futurist banquette scene by adding the necessary 'flowers' Marinetti had longed for. The scene was reversed and the predominance of the sexual regime was replaced by a privileged role played by the alimentary regime. Instead of the aestheticised white food standing as a metaphor for the white object of the black desire, the Fascists converted black bodies into prey and food 'cooked' by bombs. What was aestheticised in this case, however, was not the black body but the actual act of 'cooking' itself, with the Fascist State emerging as a kind of master chef, a 'culinary artist'. After all, as Goebbels had claimed some years earlier in his novel *Michael*, "politics are the plastic art of the State" (quoted in Jay, 1992, p. 47), the 'culinary art' we could correct him. Even though the Italian Fascists themselves did not actually employ metaphors of eating and cooking, we know that in many cases, as for instance in the US lynching culture of that same period, cannibalistic metaphors of cooking, eating and incorporation were often employed with white racists constructing the burning black bodies as food cooked in fire (see Gray, 2015).

Metaphors of eating and incorporation, even when implicit or unspoken, are endemic to the exercise of power (Canetti, 2000]. Of course, governmentality implies that there is now no need for an external power to hunt its victims. As it is, we are constantly throwing the bombs at ourselves, in turn, cooking us as 'tasty' food to be devoured. This conflation of the self/body and food is reflected in various examples from contemporary art. Photographer Blake Little's *Preservation* project, for instance, made up of a series of photo-shoots of naked bodies coated with honey, stands as a clear case of the aestheticisation and depiction of the human body as an edible object to be tasted and consumed. Thai sculptor Kittiwat Unarrom, to cite another example, makes unbelievably realistic looking sculptures of dismembered human body parts sculpted entirely from bread. In the exhibitions of his *Body Bakery* project people can cut pieces from the gruesome body parts and taste them as if eating human flesh. Similarly, Annabel de Vetten's cake-sculptures portraying realistic severed faces and mutilated body members made from chocolate and sugar brings together culinary art and an anthropophagic imaginary. Whether these artists actually violate gastropornographic fantasies and ideology, and expose in a disturbing way the hidden psychopolitical aspect of contemporary culinary culture, or whether they actually strengthen culinary and alimentary psychopolitics is indeed a moot point. However, in thinking of these visitors to Unarrom's exhibitions who cut up and swallowed 'human body parts' made of bread, or imagining the 'creatives' de Vetten identifies as her customers (Davis, 2015, n.p.) plunging their spoons into gruesome chocolate baby brain cakes, one is forced to contemplate how ominously true Benjamin's (2005) concluding lines in *The Work of Art in the Age of Mechanical Reproduction* can turn out to be: "[mankind's] self alienation has reached such a degree that it can experience its own destruction as an aesthetic pleasure of the first order" (p. 20).

Notes

1 Given the psychopolitical importance of the 'alimentary regime' as far as the intermingling of bodies and selves is concerned, alimentary and culinary metaphorics allow for explicit as well as implicit analogies linking food preparation to, say, the making of the self, or personal relationships. What is called 'Culinary Art Therapy' is an example of the culinary metaphorics of the self in practice. Culinary Art Therapy is precisely a reflection on the (care of the) self and one's relationships through analogies with the actual process of cooking a dish (see Ohana, 2008).
2 The romanticisation of key entrepreneurial personas (Jobs, Branson, Oliver, etc.) also functions as part of neoliberalism's marketing of itself. As Peroulis (2012) argues, neoliberalism romanticises its entrepreneurial 'heroes' in order to conceal the violence of financial markets under the aesthetics of the genius.
3 In a lecture bearing the title 'Commenting the inexistent seminar', Jacques-Alain Miller (1991) wonders whether we could approach the Name-of-the-Father as the name of a function, NF(x), in which the x in the brackets is a variable that depends on each clinical case. Thus, 'the Chef' could be what plays the role of the Name-of-the-Father within the alimentary regime.
4 In Chapter 6, the term 'gastroporn' is employed to describe the overlapping space between the alimentary/culinary regime and the sexual regime, and in order to discuss elements that emerge from this common territory.
5 In the Greece of economic crisis and massive unemployment and poverty, the 13th workshop on Gestalt psychotherapy organised in Athens in 2011 bore the title: 'the creative adaptation of a society in crisis', whilst the workshop organised the following year was advertised as an exploration of "how the Self, which according to Gestalt theory is in a constant process of change, becomes the *artist* of our lives" (see Mentinis, 2013, italics added). The idea of the self as an artist who creates its own existence as a work of art is thus endemic to conservative political notions of 'creative adaptation' to emerging conditions as opposed to resistance and fighting back.
6 This is a point the implications of which I will explore further in Chapter 3 where I will discuss culinary psychopolitics in Chile.

2 From the semiotic to the symbolic
Placentophagy and the name-of-the-chef

Ritualistic placentophagy

On 4 February 1998, in what became one of the more controversial episodes of Channel 4's *TV Dinners* in the UK, celebrity chef Hugh Fearnley-Whittingstall served a woman's placenta at a dinner party after he had fashioned it as a pâté; the placenta was fried with shallots and garlic, flambéed, puréed and served on focaccia bread (Channel 4, 1998). The story, as discussed in the programme and explained in subsequent interviews with the chef, goes like this: nineteen-year-old Rosie and her partner, Lee, have brought their newborn daughter, Indie-Mo, to visit their grandparents, Rosie's parents. To mark her first grandchild's birth, the grandmother together with her friend had decided to organise a party in which family and friends would be served Rosie's placenta. The idea was to intentionally set up the whole thing to resemble a ceremony that would reflect the way in which the placenta is treated in pre-modern cultures (Gibson, 1998). Indeed, the shamanistic overtones become overt in many instances during the programme: while the grandmother's friend chops up and flambés the placenta in a frying pan she exclaims: "earth and air and wind and fire, and what's all this about?" (quoted in Ashley *et al.*, 2004, p. 36). And when the placenta pâté has been prepared, Mary, the grandmother, invites the guests to try it by declaring: "here's some of our generic pool! Dive in!" (Harper's Magazine, 1999, n.p.), as if through the consumption of the cooked placenta the guests would experience a mystical delving into the biology of the visceral bond of the mother and the child.

There was, nevertheless, a canibalistic element in the stated intentions of the family that contradicted the family's adducing to pre-modern cultures. Ritualistic placenta reverence is indeed rather common among pre-modern, indigenous cultures around the world, and its proper ceremonial disposal is believed to be indissolubly connected to the biological and psychological maturation and health of the child, as well as social stability as a whole (see Davidson, 1983, 1985; Fernández Juárez, 2002; field notes, 2014). Despite the widespread practice of ceremonial burials, however, actual placenta and umbilical cord consumption is conspicuously absent in indigenous cultures (for a review of relevant literature see Young and Benyshek, 2011). Interestingly, then, the Clear family did not just simply communicate the intended ritualistic character of the placenta dinner, but had also introduced in the ritual a cannibalistic component that found no correspondence with the cultures they were honouring.

Despite the grandmother's and her friend's central role in the organisation of the commensal ritual, the female participants, in actual fact, acted as the chef's accomplices, following his specialist instructions and acting on behalf of his masculine culinary authority. That is to say, it was the figure of the celebrity chef, his symbolic function which structured the ritual, imbued it with meaning, and sanctioned the transformation of an inedible visceral organ into an edible 'magical' object. It was a significant programme inasmuch as it marked the return of the figure of the cannibal as a chef, or, alternatively, signalled the emergence of the figure of the chef as a cannibal. Sixteen years on from that ritual placenta dinner on Channel 4, Nick Baines (2014), a regular food and travel contributor to *The Guardian* – and, hence, a culinary expert authority also – inspired by the master chef Hugh Fearnley-Whittingstall, performed his own solitary, but no less spectacular, placentophagic ritual, describing in his column how he ate his wife's afterbirth raw in a smoothie as well as cooking it in a taco. In a figurative way, Baines writes in his article: "the following morning, my wife sat out of the way in the front room while I set about one of her body parts in the kitchen" (ibid., n.p.).

Taking its lead from these two examples, the purpose of this chapter is to probe into the culinary preparation and eating of the placenta and the umbilical cord, drawing especial attention to the way this form of mild cannibalism constitutes a culinary ritual, that marks a passage from the 'maternal' semiotic to the symbolic order. The chapter raises and attempts to answer the question of whether placentophagy as practised by figures of culinary authority should be read as a 'ritualistic' attempt to restore declined paternal authority, or whether it is better understood as an intervention consonant with neoliberal psychopolitical transitional demands, and structured according to the culinary metaphorics of the dominant culinary/food culture.[1]

The name-of-the-chef

A recurring central theoretical tenet in contemporary Lacanian psychoanalytic theory is that the 'Name-of-the-Father' *according to tradition* (see Miller, 2012, n.p.) has now been fractured, and devalued by the discourses of science and capitalism, resulting in the decline and collapse of the father figure as the corner-stone of the symbolic order. As a key emblem of law and order, the symbolic father figure facilitates the transition from nature to culture through the articulation of the incest prohibition, represents sexual difference in structuring the opposition between masculinity and femininity, and introduces the difference between the generations in supporting the function of the Ego-ideal. The shift from belief in the almighty father of childhood to provocation and destruction in puberty and adolescence, and the subsequent coming to terms with him in adulthood thus no longer occurs; the symbolic father functions have become questionable and collapsed (Verhaeghe, 2000).

The death of the symbolic father as the structural provider of our psychic coordinates is said to elicit a broad range of new psychosocial symptoms, ranging from substance abuse to child abuse, from vandalism, racism and full-blown gender-bending and the development of new-age spiritualism and political insurgency. It is in this gulf that separates the father's eagerness to deposit his sperm from his inability or unwillingness to act as the support of law and order, that social and psychic problems are allegedly said to germinate. Žižek (1999) writes that a father is no longer perceived as one's Ego-ideal, the bearer of symbolic authority, but, rather, as one's ideal ego and imaginary competitor; a transformation that, ultimately, precludes entry into adulthood and condemns somebody to a perpetual immature adolescence. The destruction of the father's symbolic function, Žižek (1997) argues elsewhere, has unleashed what he calls a primal anal father – a figure which is only concerned with his own *jouissance*. Thus, increasingly our world is characterised by the return of figures which function according to the logic of the 'primordial father', from totalitarian political leaders to the paternal sexual harasser on one side, to the increase of hysterical subjects who are on the run crying out for a new master.

This now widespread thesis has been challenged by Nobus (2003), who identifies a certain conservativism lurking behind the putative decline of paternal authority. Nobus argues that many prominent social researchers over the past 150 years, long before the advent of psychoanalysis, have championed the importance of paternal authority as a precondition of psychic health and social well-being, whilst holding up its decline as an explanation for a manifold range of social problems and psychic suffering. Yet, he goes on explaining, whilst certain reorganisations and transformations in Western family life may indeed have resulted in the decline of the paternal function, "paternity has at the same time always resurfaced under a new shape, defiant and rejuvenated" (n.p.).

It would be tempting at this juncture to combine the two ideas and put forward the thesis that the ubiquitous figure of the chef, and the culinary expert in general, constitutes a kind of re-emergence of paternal authority through the metaphorics of cooking; the latest in a long line of shapes paternal authority has taken in order to resurface 'rejuvenated' and 'defiant'. As such, the aforementioned examples of placenta culinary treatment would be read as shaman-esque interventions on the visceral organ that stands for the mother-fetus connection, as a ritualistic performance of separating the two, of breaking their tie of dependency, thus re-affirming and imposing, simultaneously, a symbolic order expressed as a culinary/alimentary aesthetic. In this sense, the literal eating and digestion of the placenta would also stand for the impossibility of a future mother-child re-connection, the depleting of any desire for a return to the primordial condition of maternal fusion, thus rendering the imaginary of the visceral and umbilical connections unthinkable – I will come back to this later in the chapter.

This is an idea, however, which I have already rejected in Chapter 1, coining instead the term the 'name-of-the-chef' in order to designate a function that imposes an alimentary/culinary law (and a sexual one) that facilitates a transition towards creative adaptability to neoliberal conditions, forcing the person to break from their dependency and attachment to the 'maternal' (i.e. the family, the 'nanny state', tradition, habit, etc.), and engage with the wider neoliberal symbolic. Simply put, whilst the figure of the chef or culinary authority performs the function of separation and the imposition of prohibitions in a way that closely resembles the paternal function, he is nevertheless a figure that performs a properly neoliberal transitional function. As such, he should not be understood as an expression of the re-emergence of the father authority, but rather as a figure who has appropriated a historically 'feminine' activity, that is, cooking/feeding, in order to deplete and disempower the 'feminine', the 'maternal' and impose symbolic laws on it. The placentophagy of this sort, then, should be seen as a more technical aspect of the name-of-the-chef, one that targets in more specific terms what Kristeva (1984) calls the semiotic *chora* (both in literal and metaphorical terms) in an attempt to socialise it through cooking, and thus tame it and exercise control on it.

Eating the placenta, of course, is mostly advertised by celebrity women, and is almost exclusively practised by women rather than by men. In light of this, how can we still claim that the placentophagous male culinary authority performs a function of separation from the 'maternal' or aims to control and neutralise the unruliness of the semiotic *chora*, when it is actually women themselves who increasingly eat and assimilate their own placenta and umbilical cord, 're-absorbing' in a sense the visceral connectivities and rhythms it stands for? At best, culinary placentophagy could be read as an imitation of a largely motherly practice, or a spectacular but impotent attempt to colonise such a practice. This altogether plausible objection, however, soon collapses if one looks more carefully at the rationale behind this lucrative new trend among mothers, and considers the way in which placentophagy is discursively justified by women themselves. For, in sharp contrast to male culinary experts, women explain and justify their choice to 'eat' their afterbirth through recourse to its alleged wide-ranging therapeutic properties: from its nutritional value and energising qualities to its beauty effects (e.g. smoothens facial wrinkles), and psychotherapeutic benefits (e.g. treating post-natal depression).

Despite the fact that there is often a clear awareness on behalf of these women that what they are doing is actually a form of cannibalism, albeit a mild and harmless form, the possible feelings of 'abjection', to introduce another Kristevian (1982) term I will return to later, are neutralised precisely by the use of medical/therapeutic discourses. Indicatively, Placenta Wise in the United States, one of the extremely profitable companies offering to boil, dehydrate, ground and encapsulate the placenta for women, succinctly state on their webpage: "it's not weird or freaky or gross. It's science" (Placenta Wise, n.d.). Similarly, the actress January Jones explains that placenta capsules are "not gross or witch-crafty" before going onto describe how they helped her to combat her baby blues and fatigue (quoted in Bull, 2013, n.p.). One can find countless near identical statements from celebrity mothers on the internet. If among indigenous people across the world the reverence in which the placenta is held retains a strong spiritual meaning, eating of the placenta in the Western world by women has been completely saturated by a scientific discourse, as well as implicitly by the discourse of capitalism by virtue of the fact that it has been transformed into a profitable commodity and an extremely profitable and fast-growing business. Thus, what is consumed is not the visceral organ associated with the maternal semiotic *chora*, nor does it mark an attempt to somehow re-appropriate a non-oedipalised relationship to the child, on the contrary, the placenta is re-absorbed by mothers after it has already been mediated by the discourses of science and capitalism. Thus, swallowing placenta capsules re-affirms and strengthens the power of those same discourses that are said to have brought about the decline of the Name-of-the-Father, and which are endemic, albeit in a tacit form, to the function of the figure of the (placentophagous) chef.

On the other hand, the discourse of the two aforementioned male culinary experts is characterised by a conspicuous absence of any reference to the therapeutic benefits of the placenta and umbilical cord. Rather, placentophagy is almost exclusively attributed to 'curiosity', 'experimentation', 'omnivorousness', the 'breaking of a taboo', with much of the attention being drawn to the preparation itself, with succulent descriptions of the recipes accompanied by flashy gastropornographic images of the final result. What seems to matter, above all else, is the creative endeavour by which what is initially perceived as an 'abject' object coming out of the maternal intrauterine space, is transformed through the 'magic of cooking' into an aesthetic edible delicacy (and is thus socialised). These positively valued 'personal' qualities (i.e. experimentation, creativity, curiosity, omnivorousness, etc.) are, as we saw in the previous chapter, indissolubly connected with neoliberal psychopolitical transitions.

The first person to perform this kind of spectacular placentophagic ritual on the aforesaid Channel 4 programme, Hugh Fearnley-Whittingstall – a celebrity chef as well as a graduate in philosophy from Oxford University – has been fairly explicit about the social role of the chef in shaking established views and instigating change. By succinctly justifying his culinary interventions in terms of the need for people "to be shocked" and be "reminded of things" (see Gibson, 1998; Stanford, 2011; Stadlen, 2013), and affirming that his sole intention with the placenta episode was to "breach an eating taboo" (see Gibson, 1998), Fearnley-Whittingstall thus confirmed the psychopolitical dimension of the programme. Phrased otherwise, the show's aim was not to educate in the traditional sense of transferring some important piece of information to the audience, a recipe in this case, but, rather, to "shock" and "breach" (albeit in mild and highly controlled forms) that is, to induce a destabilising effect upon a particular psychosocial configuration, and thus open up the possibility for the intrusion in it of new elements. In this case, the placenta is both the medium and the message of the culinary ritual: it is the medium by virtue of the fact that it is the actual consumption of a human organ that causes the disturbing and destabilising effects, and the message about what this is all about. Performing a reading of what precisely the message behind culinary placentophagy is, forms the basis of the rest of the chapter. In order to do this it is important I first briefly introduce Julia Kristeva's notion of the *semiotic*.

The semiotic and its *chora*

Kristeva's (1984) notion of the 'semiotic' can be thought of as describing the anarchic, pre-oedipal 'raw material' of signification, the bodily zones and organs, as well as libidinal rhythms, energies and drives associated with the maternal body. As Homer (2005) describes it, the semiotic is an "endless movement and pulsation beneath the symbolic" (p. 118), and it must be harnessed and channelled for social cohesion and regulation. Margaroni (2004) argues that the semiotic refers to an operation that logically and chronologically precedes the positing of the phenomenological subject and the establishment of its corollaries on the level of language, namely the sign and syntax, or, as Kristeva (1984) calls it, the *symbolic*. The semiotic, for Kristeva, is feminine, and a phase indissolubly connected to the maternal visceral space she calls *chora*, which, in turn, can be described as "an essentially mobile and extremely provisional articulation formed at the crossroads of language and biology through the playful transfer between two bodies: the infant's confused mass of body parts and the mother's always already socialized body" (Margaroni, 2004, p. 14). The *chora* is a kind of ordering but not a law, it is informed by socio-historical constraints but is not reduced, limited to or dominated by these constraints (Kristeva, 1984).[2] In contradistinction to the *chora*, the 'symbolic' is dominated by the law of the father; it is a domain of positions and propositions superimposed on the semiotic. The symbolic domination over the semiotic, however, is a rather tenuous and fragile one, liable to lapse and collapse at particular significant moments when the semiotic manages to surface, overflowing its boundaries. Sarup (1993) identifies these significant moments as being of three kinds: historical, psychical and linguistic, which we can understand as radical social upheavals (e.g. revolts, revolutions and contentious riots), personal dis-identifications and rebellions (madness and holiness are the examples offered by Kristeva) and art (Kristeva discusses *avant-garde* poetry).

The reason for this brief theoretical digression on the Kristevian 'semiotic' is that, since the placenta is an organ that grows inside the maternal body and defines a certain visceral relationship of umbilical connectivity between the mother and the fetus, it is an organ that exists within the semiotic *chora*, its pulsations and rhythms. In fact, it would be more accurate to claim that the placenta is the most central organ in the very constitution of the *chora*, because of the connectivity (mainly in terms of nourishment) it establishes between two 'bodies', and that its disconnection during birth and the subsequent cutting of the umbilical cord marks the dissolution of this provisional maternal space, which, nevertheless, through the placenta retains a 'mysterious', 'organic' representation in the world.

In pre-modern, indigenous cultures the placenta is usually buried unmodified and 'untouched' deeply into the earth where it decomposes and assimilates, thus strengthening the person's ties with the vast semiotic *chora* of 'mother-earth'. It is from their visceral and spiritual connection to this earthly semiotic space that indigenous movements in Latin America derive their revolutionary force, and it is precisely this relationship that neoliberal policies attempt to sever by privatising land and transforming it into a commodity (see also next chapter). In contradistinction, today's culinary culture looks to claim the placenta for the symbolic, imposing on it a culinary aesthetic, allowing it to be incorporated into the symbolic body of the culinary authority, and establishing a different relation between the 'maternal' semiotic and the symbolic. It is important to reiterate, here, that the semiotic is to the symbolic, both, an uncontrollable excess that returns to disrupt it and perform transgressive breaches on it, but also its very precondition (Kristeva, 1984). In this sense, the cooking and eating of the placenta could be read as an attempt to tame and domesticate the force of the semiotic, its excess and its disturbing effects, a kind of controlled and manageable (through cooking) unleashing of its disturbing energies, which are then channelled into producing symbolic re-configurations necessary for the expansion of the neoliberal economy.

At the same time, eating and thus incorporating the placenta within the neoliberal symbolic conveys the message that no visceral connections will be tolerated, that any imaginary connections to the semiotic would be abrogated. If, as Lorraine (1999) writes vis-à-vis Irigaray, the intrauterine space is a non-oedipal space of plenitude and the interactive attunement of the singularities, rather than the grid of social positioning that pertains to all, then, as Braidotti (2002) explains, the placenta and the umbilical cord can provide alternative figurations of intersubjectivity, with the complex symbiotic relationship between mother and child providing alternative ways of figuring interconnectedness. It is precisely these alternative ways of interconnectedness that are abrogated by subjecting the placenta to ritualistic cannibalism. Although abjection renders the imaginary functions of the placenta resistant to appropriation – indeed upon trying the placenta raw *The*

Guardian's contributor informs us that he found it "nauseating" – culinary treatment endows edibility on it. If abjection, as Kristeva (1982) argues, is the way through which every society establishes individual (and collective) boundaries, and if the first and foremost act of abjection is the rejection of the 'maternal' body, then culinary treatment and eating of the placenta stands as another instantiation of a ritualistic re-negotiation of neoliberalism's relation to the maternal.

The return of the cannibal (part two)

As was mentioned earlier, in those indigenous/pre-modern cultures around the world where the placenta is revered, the altering of its texture is strictly prohibited.[3] Among the Aymaras of Bolivia or native cultures in Mexico, for example, the placenta is buried in the earth pure, unaltered and 'untouched' (Chevalier and Sánchez Bain, 2003; field notes, 2014). Washing it or smoking it with incense – what is often mistakenly taken as a form of cooking – is meant to keep the bad spirits away and offer a kind of protection for the time it remains in the space between the maternal semiotic and the semiotic *chora* of the mother-earth, rather than inflict changes on its texture. Ungraspable and mysterious, uncanny and feared the placenta is thus buried deep enough into the earth so that animals will not find it and devour it before it is decomposed and assimilated. No living being is allowed to consume it. This is the element the Clear family in the Channel 4 programme omitted when citing pre-modern cultures, obfuscating the unusual cannibalistic character of their placentophagic ritual.

"Amidst the explosion of the current obsession with food and eating lurks a strange figure" writes Probyn (2000), "the figure of the cannibal has returned to haunt Western societies, from which, of course, it originally came" (p. 81). Probyn, as well as many other scholars writing within the thematic of contemporary cannibalism, in both its literal and metaphorical senses, situate cannibalism within consumer society, and as having a double meaning in relation to it: as both the product of the excesses of the consumer society, and a critique of it, as carrying a yearning for a limit to the seemingly endless appetites of consumer society. hooks (1992) discusses 'eating the other' as being expressive of a consumerist 'hunger' for difference, for other modes of understanding everyday life. The encounter with the other is one that carries with it the seductive promise of freeing oneself from the shackles of a fixed and static identity, from a condition of containment and death, a desire that within consumerist society is predicated upon

From the semiotic to the symbolic 37

the commodification of the other, especially the racial female other. Thus, 'eating the other' is expressive of white masculinity as a 'state of incompleteness' that needs to be supplemented with ethnic difference, which becomes a kind of seasoning that spices up the dullness of mainstream white male culture (hooks, 1992; Probyn, 2000).

As significant as these reflections undoubtedly are, they do not necessarily help us elucidate the cannibalistic character of placentophagy specifically, and, moreover, they fail to address the fact that the figure of the cannibal returns, first and foremost, as a chef. Or, phrased otherwise, it is the figure of the chef that emerges as a cannibal. That is, cannibalism returns as an endemic component of the neoliberal function of the name-of-the-chef. This is a stage beyond the classical Marxian vampiric, that is to say parasitic, relation of capital (dead labour) to living labour (see Neocleous, 2005) involving nothing less than the 'eating of the other'. The NBC TV series *Hannibal*, in which a psychopathic murderer-chef gourmetises his victims before eating them is only one of the many figurative examples of the return of the cannibal as a chef or the emergence of a chef as a cannibal. Even when 'eating the other' is used as a metaphor for white people seeking multiple 'colourful' and 'tasty' sexual experiences with the racial other (see hooks, 1992) this, as will be discussed in Chapter 5, should be situated within the workings of a gastrosexual condition that constructs women as 'edible entities', and be read in conjunction with the fact that cooking has become an important part of the male repertoire of seduction.

In *Tristes Tropiques*, Lévi-Strauss draws a distinction between 'anthropophagic' and 'anthropoemic' (from the Greek *emein*, 'to vomit') customs of social control. The first, practised among pre-modern societies, consists of the cannibalistic absorption of otherness, of alterity: "the only way to neutralize people who are the repositories of certain redoubtable powers, and even to turn them to one's own advantage, is to absorb them into one's own body" (1961, p. 386). The second, the anthropoemic, either expels or vomits otherness outside the body social or encloses it in social institutions. However, even though Lévi-Strauss deployed this distinction as a means through which to critique the intolerance of the modern world, it is somewhat doubtful whether eating the other is any more tolerant than in the anthropoemic world. Furthermore, as Young (1999) explains, without being intrinsically tolerant, late-modernity also displays anthropophagic social control by 'bulimically' consuming diversity and otherness, and symbolically embedding them in society as a potential source of profit, only to anthropoemically 'spit them out' when they are no longer necessary or displaying an 'inaptness' of conformity to their required roles. Placentophagy, then, diverting from the intentions of Lévi-Strauss's distinction, marks a controlled inclusion of elements of difference and otherness associated with the semiotic excess, and their channelling into market economy.

Placenta culinary treatment emerges as an inevitable necessity precisely because of the semiotic's unruliness to the symbolic law, its abject character. If it had been possible to intervene and affect its nature, and therefore the relationship it maintains, then any culinary treatment would be rendered obsolete, redundant and unnecessary. "I cooked a balanced, nutritious diet throughout my wife's pregnancy, interspersed with vast quantities of *chocolate digestives*", writes *The Guardian* contributor in his article, before adding an interesting comment: "sadly, none of the biscuity nuances came through in the meat [the placenta]" (Baines, 2014, n.p., italics added).[4] Is such a comment not expressive of a certain wish to exercise a degree of control over the maternal *chora*, to alter the 'taste' of the pre-oedipal space, to augment it with the 'taste' of the symbolic, and, above all, interfere in the very mother-fetus bond? Even though, as we saw earlier, Kristeva (1984) argues that the socio-historical does exert a certain kind of influence on the semiotic, this influence is limited, and the semiotic retains its rampant autonomy. It is precisely this autonomy *The Guardian* columnist comes across when failing to taste the chocolate digestives' nuance on the placenta, which retains its abject and "nauseating" taste. And it is this realisation that enjoins a culinary ritual. Yet, if after all the balanced, nutritious diet he claims to have provided for his pregnant wife it is the nuance of the 'chocolate digestives' that he looks for in the "meat" above all else, and if cooking the placenta is conducted precisely because it lacked the desired chocolate taste, then it would be fair to assume that the chocolate digestives taste must contain significant information about the meaning of his interventions.

In the Western world chocolate carries a load of cultural meaning that links it, first and foremost, to a certain economy of desire – structured around notions of sexual satisfaction, hormonal balance and psychological stability (see Taylor, 2010; Fahim, 2012; McQuillan, 2014). Having said this, if chocolate is culturally constituted as a substitute for the real object of desire, then can we not read the expectation to impose its taste on the placenta as expressive of a wish to exercise control over visceral desires, to 'substitute' them? Furthermore, the word 'chocolate' condenses a neoliberal regime of labour that registers the vicious return of all those pre-formal modes of surplus value extraction that were deemed outdated (e.g. child labour, child slavery, child prostitution, etc.), especially for non-white populations (Shah-Shuja, 2008). As the largest production of chocolate consumed in Europe comes from children's slave-labour in the Ivory Coast, *The Guardian* contributor's expectations communicates a psychopolitical wish concerning the visceral imposition and 'digestion' of this cannibalistic neoliberal 'chocolate' regime of labour; a cannibalistic regime which the placentophagous culinary experts re-enact. An adolescent black slave who managed to escape from a chocolate plantation in the aforementioned country reported to the journalist who interviewed him: "when people eat chocolate they are eating my flesh" (quoted in Sapoznik, 2010, n.p.). Chevalier and Sánchez Bain (2003) who studied placenta reverence among native Mexicans report that their informants identified a clear causal relation between the kinds of placenta treatment and one's future conditions of work. If, for instance, the placenta is burnt, instead of buried, work in the maize field will be really hard and the person will sweat a lot. It is only the placenta's 'return' to the "freshness of the earth" – representing the establishment of a visceral connection with the land – that guarantees better working conditions. It is my contention that we can read a similar shamanistic logic behind contemporary mediatic placentophagy; the name-of-the-chef imposes a certain regime of work.

The placenta as a metaphor

The 'maternal', to which I have referred at several points throughout this chapter, should not be understood necessarily in literal terms. Indeed, as Boulous Walker (1998) argues vis-à-vis Kristeva: "even though much of her work focuses on the maternal, it is not clear that Kristeva's maternal is a category that has much to do with women" (quoted in Tyler, 2009, p. 81). The same is true for the notion of the 'abject', which should neither be restricted to the level of the individual nor be understood necessarily in a literal sense. Indeed, Vice (1997) explains that this sense of 'pollution' that brings about revulsion, disgust, nausea, abjection "has nothing necessarily to do with the danger of being literally poisoned; in most cases, the threat to the subject from an unacceptable substance is metaphorical" (p. 164). Abjection can thus be defined as the negative attempt to establish individual as well as social boundaries by expelling those elements which are no longer wished to be included in the constitution of a new identity.

Thus, the 'maternal' to be 'spitted out' or 'cooked' can also be approached in metaphorical terms, as any state of intimate connections, and 'dependency' that prevents an individual or a social body from being in a trajectory of 'development' and constant change. An example of this would be the welfare state, which for neoliberal ideologues is said to create a condition of dependency in which people become unwilling and eventually unable to face up to the responsibilities of work, take the necessary risks, and make investments for the future as fully developed entrepreneurs. Furthermore, the benefits that welfare states provide for women are to be blamed for encouraging them to become single mothers, in turn, contributing towards a culture of disorder because of the inability of these single mothers to adequately socialise their children (see Young, 1999 for an exposition of this logic in American society). We are, thus, right back at the thematic of the decline of the paternal authority – which in this instance can be blamed on the welfare state's contribution to the decline of the bread-winner father – that is so prevalent in US neo-conservative thought (see also Nobus, 2003) and provides justification for the dismantlement of the welfare state. Rather than the re-emergence of the paternal figure, however, it is now neoliberalism that assumes paternal functions of separation. Within this framework, then, the placenta serves as a metaphor for a kind of visceral relation of dependence, and its culinary transformation and consumption constitutes a ritual of separation of the elements it connects; elements which vary from context to context. It is this metaphor that implicitly informs the discussion of the cases of Chile and Greece that I will now turn to in the next two chapters.

Notes

1 The reader is advised to first read Chapter 1, where the figure of the chef and his function in neoliberalism is discussed in greater detail.
2 Though the semiotic and the semiotic *chora* are often discussed in literal terms as referring strictly to the mother's body, it is important that we extend the energies and spaces they describe beyond the body. Thus, and this is something I will return to in later chapters, the maternal semiotic *chora* could be understood metaphorically as a culturally constructed feminised space of pulsation that is seen as posing a threat to the symbolic, and thus needs to be controlled and tamed.
3 An exception would be the rare instances in which the placenta is burnt. However, burning the placenta to ashes is not an actual altering of its texture but a way to accelerate its 'decomposition', and thus its re-absorption into the semiotic of the 'mother earth'.
4 We find a similar performatics of care in Jamie Oliver's assertion in *The Naked Chef*: "I didn't want Jules to feed herself on ready meals so I found myself custom-making the fantastic 'Jamie Oliver dinners in a bag' " (quoted in Hollows, 2003, p. 237).

3 From colonialism to neoliberal multiculturalism
A Mapuche spice in the Chilean national cuisine

From the battlefield to the kitchen

The Mapuche are the largest indigenous ethnic group in Chile, accounting for nearly 10 per cent of the entire population. As is the case with all indigenous groups, 'their history' begins with the arrival of the Spanish in Latin America. The history of the Mapuche, however, is different from that of other indigenous groups within both Chile and across the entire continent, as they were never defeated and conquered by the Spaniards. After ferocious battles and failing to colonise them, in 1641 the Spaniards co-signed the treaty of Quilín with the Mapuche, which established the area south of the Bio-Bio River, the Araucanía, as their territory, and officially recognised the rights of the Mapuche to independence and sovereignty (Richards, 2010; Miranda, 2013). This recognition would be lifted after Chile gained independence from Spain in 1810, and the newly created state became interested in the vast territory possessed by the Mapuche.

Even though the Mapuche were symbolically incorporated as ferocious warriors by Chilean patriots within the struggle for independence from Spain, the indigenous population refused to side with the patriots opting to maintain their autonomy instead of engaging in new wars (Bengoa, 2000). By the 1850s, mainstream political discourse in the country had shifted with the ferocious warriors now being portrayed as barbarous, uncivilised, idle and slothful people who needed to be conquered and subjugated (Richards, 2010). That marked the beginning of a long war of the Chilean state against the Mapuche, which bore the euphemistic name the 'pacification of Araucanía', and culminated in the final defeat of the Mapuche in 1883, and the usurpation of large parts of their ancestral lands by Chilean state and European immigrants (Mariman, 1990). Since their military defeat, the Mapuche have been subjected to marginalisation, racism and repression on the behalf of the Chilean state, with the only notable exception being the short-lived administration of Salvador Allende whose reforms granted significant rights to the indigenous population as well as returning usurped land (Berdichewskly, 1975 cited in Miranda, 2013).

Both the military regime that ran the country from 1973 to 1990 and initiated the neoliberalisation of the economy, as well as the democratic administrations that subsequently followed Pinochet's dictatorship, implemented policies that contributed to the marginalisation of the indigenous population, and promoted private interests over Mapuche lands (mainly logging, and other highly capitalised labour intensive farms) combined with repression. Even though the restoration of democracy did bring about some limited recognition of indigenous rights, problems still remain: the indigenous question continues to be dealt with 'by' and 'from' the state; indigenous demands for autonomy have not been addressed; and Araucanía is often the theatre for violent outbursts, as the Mapuche continue to resist internal colonialism and the presence of large national and multinational corporations operating in their areas (Mariman, 2005; Aguilera, 2012). Faced with what is a largely unresolved situation and a centuries old conflict, the Chilean state has in the last decade or so reconsidered its strategy, now opting for the rhetoric and practices of neoliberal multiculturalism in order to co-opt and incorporate the Mapuche within the country's neoliberal trajectory.

In keeping with the overall approach of this book, the purpose of the present chapter is to approach the state's effort to co-opt the Mapuche and pacify the Araucanía through culinary psychopolitics, examining the emergence of the *Cocina Chilena Renovada* ('Renewed Chilean Cuisine') paying particular emphasis to the commoditisation and nationalisation of a Mapuche condiment: *merquèn* (or *merkèn*). In its most basic form, merquèn is made with ground smoke-dried red hot chili peppers mixed with ground toasted coriander seeds and salt. The final powder has a copper-like colour, a spicy taste and a smoked odour. Merquèn is now widely used in Chile, not simply in gourmet cuisine but also as a national food seasoning present in every household kitchen, as well as being exported to various countries as a typical Chilean product. Moreover, it not only carries an economic value but, more significantly, a symbolic one, condensing a complex psychopolitical dynamic in Chilean society by expressing and constructing a transition from a past characterised by racism, exclusion and violent conflict towards a more 'inclusive' and politically stable multicultural neoliberalism.

That said, I will examine the relation between the Mapuche and the Chilean state by providing a short 'biographical' account of recent culinary trends in the country, and sketching out the social life of merquèn, as commodities, like people, have a social life and personal biographies (Appadurai, 1986; Kopytoff, 1986). Examining recent culinary developments and changes in what Potter and Westall (2013) call the 'foodscape' as well as the social life of merquèn, forces us to move beyond a strictly commonsensical economistic approach of a commodity as an item which has a use-value and an exchange-value, and instead explore the way culinary practices and products operate and 'live' in the Chilean society, and what they mean at this particular historical juncture. In this regard, questions such as where all this is actually coming from, who are the actors behind culinary innovations, how merquèn circulates, how it became popular, how it moves towards the future and so forth, all become relevant for understanding the new strategy for pacifying the Mapuche.

Given that there can be manifold kinds of possible biographies for things, each emphasising different aspects of the thing's social life (e.g. psychological, economic, cultural, historical, etc.) (Kopytoff, 1986), the account offered here does not by any means exhaust the entire foodscape and the social life of merquèn thus far. What I offer, rather, is a general overview of the Renewed Chilean Cuisine, and the social life of merquèn within its commodity phase[1] – as such, sidestepping an elaborated account of a number of other important aspects – in order to both outline the transition from a colonial to a neocolonial relation of the Chilean state to the Mapuche population, and sketch the passage from exclusionary policies to a neoliberal multicultural politics, which, in turn, expands the grip of the market upon the Mapuche in an attempt to incorporate them within a certain plan of economic development, and establish modes of peaceful conviviality. Merquèn, as I argue in the final section, is a magical substance that the state has chosen to appropriate in order to 'heal' the wounds of the past and pave the way for a future of economic 'development'.

Neoliberal multiculturalism

In the late 1970s, under the military regime of August Pinochet, Chile was the first country to undergo an extensive programme of neoliberal economic reforms, characterised by the privatisation of the public sector, deregulation of the economy, the dismantlement of the welfare state, as well as the propagation of an individualist and entrepreneurial ethos. Despite this implementation of what are rather orthodox neoliberal policies, however, the Chilean state, especially towards the late 1980s, did not operate in strictly neoliberal terms, but, rather, took the role of a 'developmental state', not unlike those states in East Asia, openly encouraging the non-traditional export sector through state sponsored subsidies and financial incentives such as tax exemptions (Schurman, 1996; Haughney, 2005). The role of exports (especially natural resource-based products derived from fishery, mining, forestry and the agricultural sectors) in the national economy grew massively, and, despite two major recessions, produced a wave of ex-professionals (business consultants, managers, etc.) turning new capitalists of the export-led economy.

Allied with the economic reforms and the financial support offered to the business sector, the state orchestrated a set of cultural reforms whose ultimate aim was to embed, diffuse and popularise neoliberal ideology and the entrepreneurial spirit within Chilean society. As Schurman (1996) writes, neoliberal discourse took a "fundamentalist" character, with all kinds of media constantly disseminating the neoliberal doctrine, with especial emphasis on development and prosperity, the individual freedoms offered by the new economic conditions, and the specific role to be played by entrepreneurs within society. This kind of extensive neoliberal propaganda and state financial support, combined with ultra-violent repression against resistance and economic brutality towards labour, allowed the spirit of entrepreneurship to take root in Chilean society across traditional social class divides.[2] This first wave of neoliberalisation took place largely at the expense of the indigenous populations, especially the Mapuche, through the massive usurpation of their lands and labour intensification in the areas they inhabited (see Vandenack, 2001; Crow, 2013). This hardline position of the state against the Mapuche would gradually change after the restoration of democracy, and it would be multiculturalism, albeit in conjunction with repression, that would develop into the new dominant mode for pacifying Araucanía.

Although multiculturalism has been promoted in Latin America by governments and sectors of civil society as an important step towards both recognising indigenous people and transitioning to a more democratic and inclusive society (which it has to a certain extent), more critical voices draw attention to the way it actually feeds into a neoliberal economy. Neoliberal multiculturalism, it is argued, characterised by a limited recognition of indigenous rights and an absence of radical change, constitutes a form of governance whose function is to achieve consent, pacify struggle, incorporate and assimilate difference, and transform culture into a marketable brand (Hale, 2002; Richards,

2010). Indeed, the case of Chile is no different in this respect. Unlike other Latin American countries, however, and despite the fact that it was the first country to implement neoliberal reforms, the recognition of cultural diversity and multiculturalism has been a painfully slow one. The words of the ex-president of the country Sebastian Piñera during his 21 May 2012 message (Chile's National Day of 'Naval Glories') is indicative of the lack of progress made until now, and exemplifies an understanding of multiculturalism as incorporation and assimilation into a certain type of development:

> we are giving a new agreement to our native people in order to integrate them in our economic and social development, and at the same time respecting their identity, culture, language and traditions. For them, we are propelling a constitutional reform that would recognise a multicultural country.
> (quoted in Navarro, 2012, n.p.)

There has thus far been no such constitutional reform. And far from recognising the Mapuche as sovereign people, the state continues to privilege neoliberal development over indigenous rights. Indeed most 'multicultural' policies concern an increase in the access of the indigenous population to the market through state sponsored programmes – mainly through the CONADI (National Indigenous Development Corporation) – which focus on the promotion and marketability of elements of the indigenous culture, ranging from eco-tourism to artisan products, to which are added value tags such as 'identity', 'traditional', 'authentic', 'ancestral' and so on (Aguilera, 2012). Following the success of its early experience, the Chilean state promotes neoliberal multiculturalism by acting as a developmental state which carefully orchestrates and choreographs its movements. As Schurman (1996) puts it, it is not the 'invisible hand of the market' that guides development in Chile, but, rather, the 'hand of the state'. It is within this context that a Renewed Chilean Cuisine has emerged in the country, with merquèn sticking out as an exemplar of an 'ethnic' culinary commodity.

Since the nineteenth century, depending on the historical and economic conditions, there have been three main representations of the Mapuche: as heroic fighter against the Spaniards; as thieves and bandits who continued fighting against the new power that replaced the Spanish authorities; as lazy drunkards who refused to be incorporated into the development projects of the Chilean nation. It is the latter two representations that inform everyday practices of racism, discrimination and paternalism against the Mapuche by the mainstream *winka* culture (the Mapuche word for designating 'whites') (Merino and Quilaqueo, 2004; Merino *et al.*, 2008). At the beginning of the twenty-first century, Aguilera (2008) argues, a fourth, positive, representation has emerged: the 'good indigenous', equating indigenous people with an ancient rich culture that forms the roots of the Chilean nation. This is a representation that neatly corresponds with the attempt to incorporate the indigenous people and their culture within neoliberal development.

This positive representation co-exists with another negative one, however. As Hale (2004) explains, the political discourse of the governments and local elites in Latin America has constructed two dichotomous versions of the indigenous people, rewarding the one found on the positive side, while condemning its Other to racialised spaces of poverty and social exclusion. On the positive end of the spectrum is the *indio permitido* ('authorised Indian') who participates in government programmes and embraces integrationist policies. Neoliberal multiculturalism incorporates indigenous people as long as they demonstrate a willingness and ability to adapt to neoliberal demands and embrace the entrepreneurial spirit – either through becoming small-scale entrepreneurs or obedient workers (see also Hale, 2002). At the other extreme lies the 'insurrectionist Indian', who struggles for the return of the usurped lands and fights for the recognition of ancestral rights and autonomy. The Chilean state, starting with the Ricardo Lagos administration in 2000, has rearticulated its former representation of the Mapuche resisting neoliberalism as not simply 'insurrectionist Indians' but as 'terrorists', responding with direct coercion and by persecuting activists under anti-terrorist legislation, which has its roots in dictatorship (Richards, 2010). Even though this dichotomisation fails to capture the complexity of the Mapuche behaviour and attitudes, it still exercises a power by forcing indigenous people to take sides with one of the two categories. Ultimately, it is those 'authorised Indians' who abandon demands of ancestral rights over land that can be incorporated within neoliberal multiculturalism, and who receive social and economic support through state sponsored training programmes and initiatives.

The 'Renewed Chilean Cuisine'

During the summit of the Pacific Alliance in the Paranal Astronomic Observatory in Chile in June 2012, upon receiving the Peruvian

From colonialism to multiculturalism 47

president, the Chilean president Sebastián Piñera (notorious for his blunders) was heard to utter the following: "the best restaurants in Santiago are Peruvian, and I am a great frequenter there". Peru, an undisputed culinary power in the region, immediately grasped the opportunity to take advantage of this 'gastrodiplomatic' gaffe. Piñera's statement was immediately splashed across the front pages and headlines of the neighbouring country: "the Chilean President admits: the best restaurants in Chile are Peruvian". In his own country the president became the target of much derision and often fierce critique at the hands of the press, who were attempting to stand up for the national cuisine. What was for all intents and purposes an informal small talk with a fellow president, thus, resulted in a major gaffe that undermined the most important cultural edifice and psychopolitical project of the last two decades in the country, the *Cocina Chilena Renovada* ('Renewed Chilean Cuisine').

The principle force behind the Renewed Chilean Cuisine has been an international association of chefs entitled *Les Toques Blanches*, which has its origins in France. In 1991, the quintessential Chilean chef Guillermo Rodríquez, founder of two of the most legendary restaurants specialising in the new cuisine in the capital Santiago (the L'Etoile in Hotel Sheraton San Cristóbal and the Bristol in Hotel Plaza San Francisco), would become officially recognised by the association and would preside over the Chilean Chapter. The purpose of the association was to develop and diffuse international gastronomy, rescue local culinary traditions, and educate people to a new culinary aesthetic through restaurants, seminars, cooking competitions and other events (Ivanovic Willumsen, 2004). The project of the Chefs of Les Toques Blanches to gentrify the Chilean foodscape with the support of the state, is most definitely a psychopolitical intervention that, first, identifies 'deficiencies' within Chilean selfhood (e.g. an inclination for the foreign, a weak identity and insufficient national pride, etc.) (see: Ivanovic Willumsen, 2004), and then sets out to overcome them by developing a new cuisine that will bring about national cohesion through both a tactical return to roots and the valorisation of native cultures, which will brand the country abroad and stimulate the economy. Indeed, over the last two decades most collectives and individual proponents of the new gourmet cuisine present themselves as 'representatives of Chile', and explain their culinary endeavours as an attempt to re-discover national identity through recourse to indigenous cultures.[3] Rodolfo Guzmán, a renowned chef and owner of the Boragó in Santiago – one of the most extravagant and, according to many food critics, the best restaurant in Chile and one of the best in Latin America – explains that:

> the world scene of haute cuisine is fantastic. But what we have tried to do is give all this up in search for our own identity. *And to do this, there can be nothing more honest than our own native people.* This is the only trend we follow.
> (quoted in Aranda, 2012, n.p., italics added)

In a similar fashion, Guillermo Rodríguez explains: "since we formed the group called Les Toques Blanches, we have tried to identify more Chilean food and *extract it from the depth of the earth* in order to achieve an identity" (2009, quoted in Aguilera, 2012, p. 53, italics added). What is interesting about both these quotations is the connection they establish between the 'search for identity' and a visceral connection to the 'earth' as somehow being connected with the native population. Guzmán is also explicit in this regard: "in our restaurant, Boragó", he explains, "we understand soil as something alive, exactly *as the Mapuche did*, the native populations of Chile. And this is something that today's society has forgotten" (quoted in Aranda, 2012, n.p., italics added).[4]

The past tense of the phrase 'as the Mapuche did' should not escape our attention here. Indeed, the Mapuche of the present, especially those inhabiting the countryside of the Araucanía, still very much think of the soil as being alive and maintain a strong spiritual connection with the earth. Let us recall a point made in Chapter 2, concerning how the semiotic *chora* of the mother-earth is the source of indigenous resistance in Latin America. As the ex-Mapuche prisoner and hunger striker (2006–2010) Lonco Juana Calfunao Paillalef explains, "should the government finally kill me, they will never in reality manage to eradicate me, *for the roots of my spirit are entwined far and deep within Ñuke Mapu* ['mother-earth'], and I will continue to return for eternity, my strength fortified manifold" (quoted in Dean, 2010, n.p., italics added). Is it not this very form of resistance fuelled by the relation of the Mapuche to the earth that the chefs exorcise from the new culinary psychopolitics? By producing a distinction between the Mapuche of the past who understood soil as alive and those in the present who, at least implicitly, are assumed not to, Guzmán does not simply reproduce a version of the state's distinction between the 'authorised Indian' and the 'terrorist Indian' we saw earlier; more than this, he claims jurisdiction over a particular understanding of the soil as alive; he simultaneously constructs

From colonialism to multiculturalism 49

and claims access to an earthly semiotic *chora* – a space-time 'society has forgotten' and describing his own involvement with it as *"acceso a lo inasequible"* (access to the unattainable/out of reach) (quoted in Aranda, 2012, n.p.) – which provides the generative force behind his work. In this way, the imaginary, exoticised, almost a-historical indigenous people somehow serve as the umbilical cord that allows him to connect with the mysteries of the earthly semiotic rhythm, and, in turn, fuel his culinary creative endeavour and the project of re-inventing Chilean identity. Precisely because these indigenous people are no longer 'real', Guzmán employs in Boragó anthropologists and biologists who together with the cooks form a research team charged with the mission of studying the practices of those indigenous people of the past, in order to 'unearth' the semiotic, aestheticise it, that is, insert it within a new constellation of taste, and then serve it to the elites and upper middle classes who frequent his restaurant. "Cuisine and nature, a harmonious symbiosis with surprising results" Guzman exclaimed (ibid., n.p.), communicating a culinary re-discovery of a native culture without natives, or at least with 'authorised natives' only.

There is, of course, nothing necessarily and intrinsically wrong about a harmonic symbiosis between nature and cooking. It is the actual and explicit intertwinement between state orchestrated neo-liberal multiculturalism and the new culinary scene that prevents us from reading such statements as merely imbued with and conveying a spirit of exoticism and romanticism, or as simply carrying a message of agro-ecological sustainability. Guillermo Rodríguez's description of the politics of his culinary projects is indicative in this respect:

> I work for Chile and for Chileans. I want my country to be recognised for having a gastronomy which is innovating, distinct, diverse, with extraordinary products. This is the idea, *continuing supporting any government*, but at the end that Chile and its people be the beneficiaries.
> (2005, quoted in Aguilera, 2012, p. 51, italics added)

At a first level of analysis one could look to situate such statements within the context of what Wilson (2011) calls 'gastrodiplomacy': an attempt to utilise national cuisine as the foundation for the creation of a national brand – a brand that promotes its culinary culture as being both world-class and distinctively Chilean. The Chef, then, acts as an ambassador of his country to the world scene by representing and promoting its culinary culture. Yet, the project of the new Chilean culinary scene as articulated by Guzmán and the chefs of Les Toques Blanches (see Ivanovic Willumsen, 2004) is not simply that of representation, but, rather, is about 'discovery', that is, the construction of a Chilean identity, and what Rodríguez's point about 'continuing supporting any government' conveys is precisely the subordination of the new culinary scene to the state's political agenda.

In keeping with what we said in previous chapters, the figure of the celebrity chef performs a properly psychopolitical function that corresponds to certain neoliberal transitional demands that go far beyond the branding of the nation, and, in actual fact, touch upon the very transformation the self, especially of the indigenous self. Guillermo Rodríguez is not simply the paradigmatic figure behind the renewed Chilean cuisine. He is the mastermind behind the 'discovery' of merquèn and its introduction within Chilean gourmet cuisine, which he did whilst working as chef in the presidential palace, La Moneda, at the time the presidents Eduardo Frei (1994–2000) and Ricardo Lagos (2000–2006) were launching a neoliberal attack against the Mapuche territory incarcerating indigenous activists under anti-terrorism laws (Aguilera, 2008). In other words, both the 'discovery' and popularisation of merquèn, and the broader project of identity construction through the re-invention of a national gastronomy which selectively and tactically incorporated the indigenous cultural heritage, literally emerged out of the kitchen of the Chilean state and was accompanied by the exclusion and/or incarceration of the 'insurrectionary', 'terrorist' Indian who defends ancestral lands. Elsewhere, Rodríguez would be even more explicit about the relation between his cuisine and state politics: "the philosophy of president Lagos", he said, "is that the table in the presidential palace should reflect what Chile is and what the Chileans are" (quoted in Aguilera, 2012, p. 153). Perhaps it would be more accurate to say that the table in the presidential palace should reflect what Chile and Chileans *should become*, but nevertheless it is important that the relations between the renewed Chilean cuisine and the state were publically communicated.

The 'discovery' and insertion of a native component within the renewed Chilean cuisine – condensed but not exhausted in the popularisation of merquèn – serves two bi-directional, albeit indissolubly connected, processes: it allows the Chilean state and the white Chileans to claim the native past – albeit an exoticised version of it as one can discern in the words of Guzmán – as the origin of the nation, and at the same time open up the doors for indigenous people to embrace neoliberal multiculturalism and be incorporated into the nation on the state's terms and conditions. We can further explore the latter dimension by posing the question what was 'wrong' with the 'old' Chilean cuisine and letting Guillermo Rodríguez respond:

> Surely, before there was also Chilean food, food *that has no representation like the Mapuche food*, which is genuinely Chilean but has *no documentation, it has no logical preparation, it has no proper assemblage* so that it can become diffused.
> (2009, quoted in Aguilera, 2012, p. 53, italics added)

The 'discovery' and 'rescuing' of the indigenous cuisine, which constitutes a fixed rhetoric of the chefs of Les Toques Blanches, involves its insertion into a different culinary constellation. It is not simply the fact that, as one chef admits, "eating like a lady in a *ruca* in Temuco is not exportable" (quoted in Ivanovic Willumsen, 2004, p. 123).[5] Besides the gentrification of the Chilean cuisine for the purposes of exportation and tourism, what is at stake here is the education of the indigenous people through the culinary metaphorics of the self.[6] Recall the words of Rodríguez that I quoted earlier in Chapter 1 apropos the initiative 'Chefs Against Hunger', in which he suggests: "these kind of initiatives allow communities to realise that they can make new recipes with the ingredients they have always used" (quoted in Via Restó, 2008, n.p.).[7] In other words, initiatives of this kind are not about tackling material poverty, but, rather, tackling poverty as cultural stagnation, repetition, habit, lack of rationalisation, and the way to do this is to re-assemble raw materials, combine them in different ways, and make new recipes. Is this not what is also expected from the indigenous people, that is, to be 're-assembled' as part of a broader transition towards being incorporated into the new multicultural neoliberal reality?

The psychopolitics of ethnic cuisine

Already from the mid-nineteenth century, the homogenisation of the country was a process that passed through the adulteration and the elimination of the Mapuche ethnic character, and, more specifically, through a 'civilising' process that entailed their transformation from indigenous to poor *campesinos* ('farmers') (Bengoa, 2000). Following suit, a law during Pinochet's dictatorship which promoted the breaking up of Mapuche land into smaller pieces and its privatisation, also established that, once privatised, owners would no longer be considered indigenous (Richards, 2007). This forced transition from being indigenous to being identified as a farmer has been gradually reversed with the transition to democracy. Multicultural neoliberalism has re-discovered the 'indigenous' and the 'ethnic' as a source of profit, and has promoted the re-invention of indigenous identities in ways consonant with the market (see Yudice, 2004). This is what Briones (2002) has called *blanqueamiento* ('whitening'), a state orchestrated strategy which has attempted to make the Mapuche less Mapuche. This 'whitening' is normally predicated upon the loosening of community ties (albeit promoting community as a spectacle for ethno-tourism), the cultivation of individualism through the promotion and funding of entrepreneurial activity, and the offering of promises of upward mobility and individual success (see also Richards, 2007). Culinary interventions of various kinds constitute the principle means through which this 'whitening' process is taking place in contemporary Chile, and it involves the teaching of a new logic of doing things and a re-invention of the self. On the one hand, the chefs of Les Toques Blanches have given a number of seminars and classes across the country, as well as cooperating with Mapuche chefs in Araucanía by giving active support to the restaurants owned by the latter in an attempt to transform the country's foodscape and diffuse the new cuisine (Ivanovic Willumsen, 2004). On the other hand, state sponsored culinary projects and multicultural programmes of various kinds have allowed the Mapuche to gain access into the new psychopolitical culinary reality.

The Guacolda High School in the Mapuche populated town of Cholchol is one of the intercultural schools (Mapudungun, the Mapuche language, is compulsory). The school, as part of its intercultural programme, also offers training in Mapuche cuisine and fusion cuisine (what is called 'intercultural alimentation') having as its objective to "revive and revitalise the Mapuche culture" (Educar Chile, 2013). Indeed, it takes little effort to understand how 'revitalisation' and 'reviving' constitute a rhetoric that feeds into the transformation of indigenous culture into a source of profit. Furthermore, it is also interesting to note the fact that indigenous cuisine is taught to the students alongside fusion cuisine, which creatively combines elements from different culinary traditions. In other words, indigenous culinary culture is revitalised by being incorporated as another dimension of fusion cuisine, as another source of inspiration as it were. In relation to the culinary training offered in the school, the cooking professor Jessica Ortega explains that:

> the idea is that every student can recognise the tastes/flavours of his/her family, try others, and that we do not just *professionalise*

the preparation of the recipes of the parents and grandparents, but at the same time we rescue traditions of the traditional cuisine which are getting forgotten.
(quoted in Red de Escuelas Líderes, 2014, n.p., italics added)

Despite the fact that the professor does not produce a causal connection, we can claim that it is actually through the 'professionalisation of the preparation of the recipes', that is, their creative modification and re-invention, and the formalisation and rationalisation of the techniques and aesthetics of presentation, that the 'rescuing' of culinary traditions is performed. Mapuche recipes are not forgotten or lost; they are part of the everyday reality of the countryside (Aguilera, 2012) and it is from there that the high school students collect them, as the professor herself admits (Red de Escuelas Líderes, 2014). What these recipes lack is 'professionalisation', or what Guillermo Rodríguez in an earlier quotation defines as 'documentation', 'logical preparation,' 'proper assemblage'.[8] Oblivious of the consonance of her discourse with state orchestrated neoliberal multiculturalism and the co-option strategies, the professor refers to merquèn and other indigenous products, arguing that:

All this food, which I know *is highly valorised in other places*, it has to be also in our countryside and cities, and for this we have to reinforce knowledge of it in the kids who carry it in their blood, and they can go on passing it on.
(ibid., n.p., italics added)

Given that these 'other places' where Mapuche products are valorised are none other than the gourmet restaurants of the renewed Chilean cuisine located in the capital and big cities, and accessible only to the upper middle classes and the elites – not to mention that in these places Mapuche products are actually 'valorised' by being repositioned, creatively mixed and combined and inserted into altogether different constellations of taste – can we not read in the professor's words a certain call for a diffusion of this new culinary logic to the wider Mapuche population? What the professor does, and by extension the multicultural school also, is to promote the re-invention of Mapuche culture, thus reproducing the 'adding value to the cultural' rhetoric which, as Aguilera (2012) observes, is endemic to the deepening of neoliberalisation within Chile and Latin America generally under the rubric of 'development with identity'. The professor gives more information about the culinary training:

when I arrived at the high school, the kids aspired to work only in precarious refectories, where they did their internship. So, the first thing I did was to get access to better places so that they could go on learning.

(Red de Escuelas Líderes, 2014, n.p.)

These better places, which, as she goes onto explain, are hotels and restaurants, are not directly related to the Mapuche culture, and what students learn there are not traditional recipes, but new techniques, and a whole repertoire of creative fusion together with a particular ethic of hard work and administration skills. Intercultural culinary training, thus, becomes a promise of upward mobility: to be a chef is synonymous with learning the skills for abandoning the past and being able to imagine a future in different terms. Since the very beginning of the emergence of multiculturalism in Chile, multicultural education has been directed towards infusing the indigenous population with an entrepreneurial spirit, with its goal defined as the promotion of a competitive spirit under 'equal opportunities' (Schild, 2000, Richards, 2010). Ana Epulef, a Mapuche cook/owner of La Ñaña, a cultural centre in the Mapuche populated town of Curarrehue where vegetarian Mapuche food is served, describes her trajectory as follows:

I started working in a vegetarian restaurant owned by foreigners. I learned everything, *including management and administration*. I was happy but a question was spinning in my mind, '*why not do the same with things from my community*' ... there came the idea of starting my own restaurant, a place with local food and local people.

(quoted in Gatica, 2008, n.p., italics added)

The entrepreneurial wish to 'do her own thing', thus, only emerges once she has gained the requisite culinary knowledge, knowledge in 'management and administration', as well as knowledge that state funds are available for precisely these purposes. Indeed, she opened La Ñaña in 2005 after applying for and getting a state funding for new indigenous entrepreneurs wishing to start a business in their communities. Failing to recognise the subtle ways through which neoliberal mentality ('doing my own business') entered her life and the life of her community, the cook, then, reproduces a state rhetoric structured around a notion of 'authenticity' apropos the Mapuche culture, which, nevertheless, she describes as a process of innovation. For instance, after discussing the indigenous people's close ties with the cycle of nature and the earth, and explaining that Mapuche food is based on what "the forest offers" and that in the winter, when there is very little to collect, meat is the staple food, she then goes on to admit that her restaurant is actually vegetarian (just like the one where she used to work, which was owned by foreigners), before subsequently adding: "in La Ñaña we practically cook no meat, this is something that calls the attention of our customers. They find it curious to be satisfied with vegetarian dishes" (ibid., n.p.). But if the customers are surprised it is precisely because vegetarianism is completely alien to the indigenous reality, because in the winter there is little to collect from the forest. Consequently, rather than authentically serving Mapuche food as she claims, what she actually does is innovating, creatively modifying traditional cuisine, in turn, distancing herself from what the forest offers, that is to say from nature, and inducing the community with a different 'vegetarian' mentality, as well as, of course, contributing to the development of 'ethno-tourism' in her area by responding to potential tourist demand for vegetarian food.

Merquèn therapy for the nation

Merquèn is the taste that dominates the adventures of the new Chilean cuisine, and it has thus come to be an emblematic product in this respect. Its native status as well as its crossing of the boundaries of the indigenous reality, its ascension from the 'low' cuisine of the poor to the haute cuisine of the presidential palace and the restaurants of the elites, its popularisation within the entire Chilean society, and its transformation into a successful and 'authentically' Chilean product for exportation, function as a metaphor for the transformation of the indigenous, and contain a promise of a better future and success for those indigenous people willing to undergo a transformative process and embrace the entrepreneurial spirit. The 'discovery' of merquèn by haute cuisine chefs has been accompanied by thorough state planning and financial support, and from the very beginning involved processes that deeply transformed the indigenous reality, such as the rationalisation of production and technical training, the imposition of certain standards of hygiene, the acquisition of a market-oriented mentality, etc.

Between 2006 and 2007, the Foundation for Agricultural Development (FIA) of the Ministry of Agriculture funded a project of study centred on the standardisation of production, commercialisation and exportation of merquèn. The responsibility for the project lay with the Department of Agronomy at the Catholic University of Temuco, and its general purpose was to improve traditional products and increase their value in the market, while supporting small producing businesses run by Mapuche. In order to ensure the success of this project, the Mapuche families who participated in the project were constantly supervised by both the professor in charge and her students, who guaranteed that the producers had abandoned their communal practices and had adopted, among other things, a different style of work and the hegemonic health and safety standards (Aguilera, 2009). The introduction of this entrepreneurial spirit demanded a certain distancing from community practices and habits. Once collected, chilies were processed and converted to merquèn at the university, and then sold to Chilean Gourmet, a company specialising in gourmet ethnic products. At a later stage, small processing plants were installed in various selected areas so that the producers could continue producing merquèn and sell it in small markets (ibid.). With more than a little helping hand from the state the new spirit of entrepreneurship turned merquèn into its spiritual force, as an ever expanding range of products containing merquèn appeared in the national market as well as abroad (olive oil with merquèn, beer with merquèn, chips with merquèn, cheese with merquèn and so on).

If, as Kopytoff (1986) argues, the social life of things conflates with people's identities, then through the social life of merquèn we can trace a significant transition taking place at the levels of the Mapuche identity and its social life. As the anthropologist Isabel Aguilera (2012) observes, in relation to the 'elegance' often attributed to merquèn, this is not a quality that the chefs associate with merquèn itself. On the contrary, in order to be incorporated within haute cuisine, merquèn needs to be 'surrounded', 'combined', 'assembled' and presented together with other elements. In the discourse of these innovating chefs, she explains, merquèn remains tied to a strange rusticity and only becomes sophisticated through "contamination" or "contextualisation", that is, through the creative work that transforms rusticity into elegance. The same is true for the indigenous people themselves; a whole new life of prosperity and success is only promised to those who will show a willingness and aptitude to embark on the project of steeping and contextualising themselves in the emerging conditions.

Yet, merquèn has acquired a powerful symbolic force, the significance of which crosses the boundaries of the Mapuche world, and touches upon the entire Chilean society. As a gastronomy columnist wrote in the magazine *Mujer*, merquèn is not a passing fashion but a product of "national pride" (cited in Aguilera, 2012). Despite the fact that it maintains a certain relation to indigenous culture, it can be asserted with certainty that it no longer belongs to any particular group. Its aura cathects and engulfs everybody, all Chileans, uniting them under its spicy flavour. Merquèn is now an indispensable material within all home kitchens, an element that allows one to feel a certain creative freedom in one's culinary adventures. It is a kind of spirit that animates food, gives it life and character; it is a magical powder that allows Chileans to perform a rite of passage from a conflict ridden divided society of the past to a new united multicultural nation of 'equal opportunities' and neoliberal 'development'.

The use of the word 'magical' to describe merquèn should not be understood necessarily in metaphorical or poetic terms. Merquèn does not derive its power only by virtue of its privileged status within the new culinary milieu and/or its association with the ethnic 'as brand'. Rather, it is also deeply embedded within a magical web of meaning that permeates the whole of Chilean society. Its main component, *aji* (red hot chili pepper) is involved in a number of syncretic, quasi-magical ceremonies, like the *santiguado* that aims to keep away bad spirits and remove the evil eye; ceremonies that are by no means restricted to indigenous groups. A company that makes tea fusions has included merquèn in its most popular energising fusion mixture, which bears the name *secretos de la machi* ('machi secrets'). Considering that 'machi' is the Mapuche word for 'shaman', one can immediately see how a shamanistic/magical imaginary is employed in order to construct merquèn as having magical properties and 'energising' effects for the people and the nation as a whole.

Furthermore, merquèn is invariably associated with the therapeutic properties of *aji*, and is widely advertised for the analgetic effects of the *capsaicin* it contains – that which gives it its spicy flavour. As an internet site selling merquèn informs its potential customers, capsaicin increases the production of the enzymes *collagenase* and *prostaglandins*, which contribute to the reduction of pain and inflammation, and causes the release of endorphins that produce "euphoria and desire to socialise" (Alimentació Sana, n.d.). In other words, merquèn emerges as a fetishised commodity in both a Marxian sense as that which obfuscates the conflictual relations between the Mapuche and the state, as well as in a more literal sense as the 'magical/therapeutic powder' of a national culinary ritualistic transaction, that aims to exorcise the colonial past, heal wounds and traumas of the postcolonial present, unite all Chileans under the spirit of entrepreneurship, and fuel the neoliberal future of the country.

Notes

1 What is implied here is a processual model of commoditisation, in which objects move in and out of the commodity state (see Appadurai, 1986; Kopytoff, 1986). Indeed, merquèn has not always been an exchangeable, sellable commodity. Before starting making its way into the commodity phase, it was a hand-made spice destined for household consumption and use in religious rituals, and hence was not available for sale.
2 By 'entrepreneurial ethic' I do not mean only the active investment, but, rather, an entire set of attitudes that support it, including certain forms of labour and work ethic.
3 On a national level, the passage from a certain socio-political condition to another is almost always accompanied by the creation of a cuisine that contributes to identity formation and national unity. From the very formation of nation states in fifteenth-century Europe to the transition to a post-colonial era of independence in Asia, Africa and Latin America, to the post-communist regimes in Eastern Europe, food is deeply involved in the cultural politics of change. Culinary practices and habits transcend their relation to the biological need for food, and become ideological practices aiming to give form to the new psychosocial reality (Mennell, 1996; Palmer, 1998; Kifleyesus, 2004; Guy, 2005; Cwiertka, 2006; Cusack, 2010; Sengupta, 2010; Tominc, 2014).
4 This tendency is also present in various forms in other countries. Potter and Westall (2013), for instance, explain in relation to the UK how BBC programmes like *Great British Food Revival* use ruralised farmhouse visuals alongside a peculiarly military call to action to support celebrity chefs' claims to rediscover the heritage food of a non-identified culinary golden age.
5 *Ruca* is the Mapuche word for 'house'.
6 The reader is advised to read Chapter 1, where the culinary metaphorics of the self are explained in more detail.
7 The politics of this initiative is discussed in greater detail in Chapter 1.
8 I do not mean to argue that the Mapuche are entirely oblivious to the role of the state in funding development programmes in their communities. Even the Mapuche who work for the state often attempt to negotiate their role as state functionaries and their Mapuche identity, showing awareness of the nature of the state's interventions and attempting to justify their own actions as contributing to Mapuche autonomy and recuperation of territory (see Richards, 2007). For example, Pablo, a social worker in a multicultural hospital of private status, but almost exclusively funded by the state (indirectly a state worker) explains his involvement with state-funded initiatives as follows:

> I could work at CONADI, but I do not because CONADI is a state apparatus to control Mapuche people. However, I encourage people to apply for the programs [that fund community initiatives] at CONADI and help Mapuche communities write proposals because we Mapuche need to use every mean to take back what we have lost to the Chilean state. I promote state programs in Mapuche communities because we need that resource. But I do not think I work for the state. I use the state for the Mapuche people.
> (quoted in Richards, 2007, p. 1329)

Besides this awareness, however, the rhetoric of the 'good Indian' who aspires to improve their life and the life of their community, and the 'terrorist Indian', as well as the poverty of the Mapuche communities, force people to take sides and accept government funding. Furthermore, the profound changes which culinary initiatives, programmes and projects induce within communities and people's understanding of things are rarely adequately understood. Culinary interventions prove to be the most effective ideological apparatus for bringing about a distancing from community habits and customs, and infuse people with a neoliberal logic of doing things, while at the same time presenting the whole endeavour as a strengthening of tradition and indigenous identity.

4 From East to West
Economic crisis and the cooking of the new Greeks

Between Constantinople and Brussels

The emblem of the Byzantine Empire – the same as the one found on the flag of the Greek Orthodox Church – is a two-headed black eagle, with its two heads looking outwards in opposing directions. One head looks out over the East, the other looks towards the West, or so it is said. As such, the emblem is assumed to define Greece's position in the world. Whether it be in terms of mentality, morality, food and music, or religion, the country has been diagnosed as suffering from a perpetual crisis of identity, a conflict between two traditions, a schizoid-existence between the East and the West.[1] It is beyond the scope of the present chapter to chart the full historical development of this condition of hybridity, but one can trace its origins back to the emergence of the Byzantine Empire after the dissolution of the Roman Empire. Constantinople's[2] capture by the Franks, namely the west Europeans, the crusaders, and the attempts to Latinise (i.e. Westernise) the population, as well as the constant attacks by the Turks and the final capture of the city by the latter in 1453,[3] define a space that ever since has been claimed by two distinct and incompatible forms of life: on one side, the mysterious, savage, traditional, Islamic and resolutely hostile East which invariably threatened the country's sovereignty and, on the other side, the modernised, rational, Christian and similarly hostile West.[4]

Byzantium was from its inception a strange mixture of Eastern and Western elements. Having Greek as its official language, culturally it bore a closer affinity to Eastern modes of being, while its state structure was closer to the Roman one. The Ottoman Empire, which succeeded the Byzantine Empire, introduced within what would later come to be defined as Hellenic/Greek space more Eastern elements, while the gradual detachment from the Empire, and the eventual war of independence in 1821, clearly implanted within the Hellenic space enlightenment ideas from the West (see Liakos, n.d.). In the twentieth century, several episodes would strengthen even more resoundingly the Eastern character of the country, just as several other episodes would also strengthen its Western character.[5] In the 1980s – with the winds of change brought to the country by the socialist government, and with an irresolute place in the EU – all this was cast in a very positive light by intellectuals, who argued that this peculiar national spatiotemporal 'entrapment' in a space-time between Constantinople and Brussels afforded the country a unique geo-cultural asset that could lead it to interesting paths, and endow it with an important role on the world stage. Greece's role as a bridge between the East and the West promised a bright and prosperous future. In this respect, it appears something went seriously wrong.

In February 2012 – with Greece now a full member of the EU but under constant threat of expulsion due to its messy economy – a well-known young, pretty and successful actress gave an interview to a women's tabloid magazine where, among other things, she stated the following: "we, the Greeks, have no class. We are uneducated. We try to pretend we are European[6] while in fact we are just Eastern" (Papacharalampous, 2012, p. 26). In the same magazine, a similarly well-known young, handsome and successful actor, upon being asked if a revolution is what the situation calls for in Greece, replied succinctly: "Greeks have to become respectful and humble, we are people with lots of complexes" (Totsikas, 2012, p. 32) – a form of psy-speak emblematic of the relatively recent psychologisation of Greek society, and the personification of the pseudo self insight described by Lasch (1991) in the *Culture of Narcissism*. These statements should not be all too readily dismissed as nothing other than the personal dissatisfaction of a couple of national celebrities. On the contrary, such phrases typify the desire of a new generation of the so-called creative class, certain sectors of the elites, the urban high-middle class to wholly abandon the country's hybridity, and undergo a programme of complete Westernisation; a process which, as the two actors explicitly mention, requires the radical and profound transformation of the 'Greek self', as well as broader cultural reform.

What is important to stress right from the start, is that for the sectors holding such views, the East comes to encapsulate an assortment of heterogeneous baggage that must be left behind. In a form not that altogether different from what Said (2003) described as 'Orientalism', 'East' is tantamount to a lack of education, conservative, traditional values, a lack of hygiene, unresolved psychological complexes within the self, immaturity and a childish faith in radical leftist politics, i.e. a political immaturity that is unable to face reality and accept that capitalism is the only possible reality. In short, 'East' is everything that lies outside 'civilisation': out with the idealised phantasmatic image of capitalism as the system of unbridled individualism, infinite growth and endless progress. After all, corruption, lack of meritocracy (another discourse wholly in the service of individualism), favouritism, bribing, in short, everything that has been associated with Greece's near bankruptcy, and economic crisis are all classified as the product of an Eastern mode of social and political relations, as well as the result of an incomplete, deficient and immature self, which derives its premises not from personal capacities and skills, but is rather hetero-determined, relying heavily on family and networks of acquaintances (see Blue, 1992). This is schematically the 'political' perception of certain sectors of the population; a class specific perception which attempts, through its constant reproduction in the mainstream media and its strengthening from various forms of psychology and the mediatic tutelage of conservative intellectuals, to impose itself as the national self-perception and paradigmatic form of reflexive self-critique. The Greek economic crisis is a depoliticised crisis, and more specifically a culturalised crisis, in the sense that what is a systemic phenomenon is reduced to the cultural characteristics of the Greek people (Žižek, 2010; Lyrintzis, 2011; Mylonas, 2012). What is said to be needed, then, is a radical transformation of the 'Greek self', namely, its transformation into a fully Westernised self.

Stelios Ramphos, a philosopher with a special affinity for Plato, is a prominent conservative intellectual whose portrayal of the Greek self, and his conceptual insights into the Greek psyche, both inform and theoretically buttress a public discourse that depoliticises the crisis, and instead reduces it to the aforementioned problematic, or what he calls the 'sick hybridity' of the Greeks: "we are no longer East either, this is why we are sick … a sick hybrid" (2011, p. 70).[7] Ramphos's case is not an individual one; indeed, he is representative of that class of ex-leftists who have not only changed camps but have also become passionate enthusiasts/apologists for neoliberal economic policies. As such, people like Ramphos serve as ideological reminders and 'proof' of the futility of leftist politics, of the need to leave behind the 'political immaturity' of youth and embrace the pragmatic-consensualism that defines the present order of things. It comes as no surprise, then, that Ramphos is the favourite intellectual of the media, and equally adored by the upper classes within the population (including journalists) who can afford to attend his rather expensive seminars. What makes his depiction of the Greeks even more important, however, is the close relation he maintains with the executive power – he was an ex-advisor to the 'socialist' Prime Minister (George Papandreou), the very man who brought the IMF to Greece, and signed the memorandums of extreme austerity measures and poverty –and his anthropology both informs and provides justification for the government's policies (see Vatsinas, 2012). Or, phrased otherwise, Ramphos is the public intellectual whose arguments legitimise neoliberal reforms and austerity measures at the level of the public's consciousness; he is the theoretician par excellence of a form of psy-discourse which contends that what needs to be changed is the Greek psychological makeup itself – a position echoed by the two aforementioned actors. For Ramphos, "it is when looking deeper that [Greece] is not Europe, but dynamically speaking, it is keen on being Europe. That is, our 'psychology' is not [European] but our ambition is [to be European]" (2011, p. 68). Suffice to say that having no European 'psychology' whilst having a strong ambition to be European, leaves one with no other option than to change one's 'psychology' in order to meet the ideal of one's ambition. This is precisely what is at stake in Greece in the years of crisis.

According to Ramphos (2011) there are several things the Greeks must change, all of which signal a transition from 'Eastern' or hybrid characteristics to 'Western' ones: they have to learn how to be less emotional and develop their rational mind, they must abandon their obsession with the past and become future oriented, break with familial links and rely on their own capacities, skills and knowledge, and so on and so forth. Of course, said argument proceeds, what is also required is a radical change in the cognitive system of the Greeks, for instance in the way they attribute causality. The tendency of the Greeks to attribute their misfortune to external causes (e.g. the four hundred years of occupation by the Ottomans, the hostile Americans and so on) is futile and covers over the personal responsibility all Greeks have for what is happening in the country. This radical personalisation of responsibility, and the simultaneous demand for individual change, inevitably leads to a radical depoliticisation of the Greek predicament, and underpins a wider political project of 'educating' and disciplining the Greeks (Vatsinas, 2012). Ramphos is perfectly clear in this respect, there has to be a profound change in two indissolubly connected aspects: the cultural and the personal; a change, moreover, that should be conceptualised and orchestrated by the media and the ministries of education and culture. The first, namely the cultural change, will put an end to the endless pretence of being 'European', and will make being 'European' an actual reality. The second, namely the radical change of the Greek self, refers to the 'education' the Greeks must undergo in order to acquire the requisite qualities needed to achieve a fully fledged 'Western' individualism (ibid.) – this is precisely the meaning that 'education' comes to take, for what the Greeks are believed to be lacking is not formal education,[8] but the psychic and mental qualities associated with 'Western' forms of selfhood, and with a functional neoliberalism. In the remainder of the chapter I will discuss this systematic attempt to 'educate' the Greeks and bring about a change in the 'national selfhood', by focusing on recent transformation in the national culinary and dietary habits and by performing a reading of two very popular Greek movies that deal explicitly with the thematic of food and cooking.

Cooking the Greek self

A Touch of Spice (2003, dir: Tasos Boulmetis)[9] tells the story of a Greek family (and can be read as an analogy for the Greek community as a whole) which is deported from Istanbul in the early 1960s due to the escalation of tension in Turkish-Greek relations as a result of the political conflict in Cyprus. The story unfolds though the eyes of the adult son of the family, Fanis Iakovidis (Giorgos Horafas), then a child and now an astrophysicist and a talented cook with a passion for traditional Greek-Turkish cuisine. The memories of the protagonist are defined by the family gatherings in Istanbul, that involved the collective preparation of food by the extended family, as well as the details of recipes of various dishes and the philosophy of cooking taught to him by his grandfather: food is a whole world, a whole universe, this is why, the grandfather explains, the word " 'g-astronomy' contains the word 'astronomy' ". While a whole host of Greeks leave Turkey for Greece, the grandfather refuses to leave and stays forever in Istanbul. Despite promising several times to visit his family in Athens, he always fails to do so. The grandfather thus represents the part of Hellenism that forever remained in the East. On the other hand, the adventures of the family in Greece, and the training they have to give their young son in order to adapt to the ideals of life in Athens during the years of the dictatorship (1967–1974), nicely captures the gradual process of Westernisation. The advice given to the parents by a high-ranking officer in the military police illustrates this point: they are to prohibit their son from spending time in the kitchen cooking, and they are to force him to adopt the 'Greek' accent (as opposed to the Eastern accent). Despite the fact that the film expresses strong nostalgia for the fully Eastern way of life left behind, it still manages to effectively capture the character of the Greek life over the last five decades: that is, the (Middle) Eastern character and rich tradition of Greek food, as well as the not wholly Westernised Greek self, which is interwoven within strong extended family webs – a self highly hetero-determined and defined by its social relations.

Greece, like all other neighbouring countries in the region, has a very rich cuisine – most of it of (Middle) Eastern character – with a huge variety of main dishes, salads and dips circulating on the family table throughout the year, obeying idiosyncratic preferences, as well as religious patterns (e.g. Lent, special fasting days, etc.). Over the preceding decade, however, Greeks have experienced a frenzy of cooking 'education' (not unlike other countries in the West) with dozens of food related TV programmes, cooking reality shows and dozens of magazines and books bombarding them with recipes, cooking techniques and other culinary tips. The question raised here, then, is what an extensive culinary education of this sort could mean for a country with such a rich culinary and alimentary tradition. We can attempt to answer this question by examining the content and form this training invariably takes. For most of the programmes concern not the reproduction of traditional cuisine – that would be of no interest after all – but either the re-making and re-invention of it or, more often, the creation of previously unknown dishes, dips and salads. The Greeks, then, are taught how to distance themselves from tradition, how to cook in a different, creative style and way; how to create dishes, not just reproduce recipes.[10] This distancing from tradition, which is not simply related to issues of self-image and body-image, but to one's desirable social status-image, is reflected also in the fact that the culinary training of younger generations does not take place as much as it used to in the context of the family (a tradition reproduction unit) but is performed by the media (see also Triliva, 2010, for a debate on such issues in relation to the island of Crete).

As I discussed in the introduction of this book, according to Lévi-Strauss (1983), the uniquely human act of cooking, that is, the transformation by fire of the raw material into cooked food provides a metaphor for the relationship between nature and culture. Furthermore, Harpur (2009) argues that initiation ceremonies in several tribal communities and cultures very often include an element of 'cooking' the person: in steam, in smoke, in hot water, etc. adding that "we cook ourselves at moments of biological crisis in order to transform ourselves from natural beings into social beings" (p. 94). It is my argument, then, that the kitchen training and culinary education to which the Greeks have been subjected over the last decade or so constitutes precisely such a rite of passage: a passage from tradition to modernisation; a passage from the 'savageness' and 'naturalness' of the East to the 'civilised' life of the West. After all, cooking in a 'Western' fashion not only means to acquire a set of 'Western' habits. More than this, it involves becoming another person altogether, a person who leaves behind the repertoric repetition of tradition and employs his/her creative skills towards innovation and bringing to life new forms. Thus, 'Westernisation', in this respect, stands for the 'creative' distancing from tradition and the embedding of culinary and dietary habits into the terrain of privatised creativity and individualism which in turn informs the culinary metaphorics of selfhood.[11] It is a rite of passage from an immature, dependent 'childhood' (of the East) to mature adulthood (of the neoliberal West). For, as Harpur argues, without a "cooking initiation we are all in danger of remaining immature, dependent, self-centred, uncertain of who we are" (ibid., p. 96). In short, all the 'deficiencies' the Greeks are diagnosed as suffering from by foreigners and local ruling elites alike.

We know from Norbert Elias (2000) that eating habits are indissolubly connected to particular forms of self and social relations. Thus, Greek (Middle Eastern) food, with its distinctive smell and taste (e.g. garlic) and the bodily odour it produces, as well as the frequent and excessive bodily eruptions that often accompany its consumption, is related to relations of proximity between bodies that are increasingly rendered repulsive, 'unhygienic' and associated with violations of personal space and feelings of disgust – processes related to the topos of the immune body, the atomised, clearly demarcated body that stands in conflict with other bodies (see Papadopoulos, 2011).[12] A fully fledged individualism requires that bodies are distant, separated. The alteration of the Greek (semi-collective) self, then, requires a change in the relations between bodies which, in turn, as we know from Deleuze and Guattari (1987), are indissolubly connected to changes in the alimentary regime. This change in the relations between bodies has been actively promoted by EU officials, through the imposition of relevant policies. For example, a regulation implemented several years ago demanded, among other things, the prohibition of hand-made products, such as cheese and sausages, from being sold to restaurants or anybody else, under the auspices of public health protection rhetoric. What was primarily at stake was not simply an interest in public heath per se, but the promotion of a business mentality, the imposition via the force of the law of a spirit of entrepreneurship: everything, from cheese to wine, had to be produced in small licensed and EU standards approved meeting plants with proper machinery (bought from

Western countries). The attempt to impose entrepreneurial mentality, however, re-calibrated also the relations between bodies. If handmade products like cheese literally contain the body of the producer: his/her hand, then, these kinds of policies ensured that the 'hand' is removed from 'hand-made' products.

On an empirical level, and on a certain level, culinary re-education seems to be working – albeit with plenty of variation from place to place and distinct class-based characteristics. For since the appearance of this food wave, there have been immense changes in the composition of the Greek table, especially the celebratory table of the younger generations of middle class families. Despite the fact that the everyday family table remains 'traditional' – albeit with several 'creative' modifications and add-ons – the celebratory table, that is, the lunch/dinner prepared on various special occasions for friends, relatives and colleagues has been recognisably 'Westernised'. For example, the traditional meat dishes with a strong taste of garlic, common to the Eastern Mediterranean coast, have given way to cosmopolitan fusion meat dishes with fruits and nuts, or self-styled spaghetti dishes. The tourists' favourite Greek salad with olive oil has been deemed embarrassingly folkloric for special occasions and has been pushed aside by the previously unknown pasta side-plates, or the rocket, parmesan, prosciutto and dried tomatoes combinations with a vinaigrette dressing. Moreover, the vegetable pies have been replaced by the outlandish and recently imported 'quiche Lauren', whilst the similarly recently imported and impressively tricolored 'cheese cake' has replaced the traditional semolina tray pies and filo pastry cakes with honey-made syrup and an often strong scent of cinnamon.

Yet, in strictly alimentary terms we could say that the 'problem' still remains. Due to the fact that the everyday dinner table remains largely 'traditional', the Greeks still appear to be somehow masquerading in public as something which they are not, at least not whole-heartedly: that is, in private, they remain distinctly Eastern (although not totally Eastern); whilst in public they behave as Westerners (although not totally Western either). One is reminded again of the aforementioned words of the actress: "we try to pretend we are European, while in fact we are just Eastern". Furthermore, in the midst of the economic crisis that affects the lower middle classes and the working classes more acutely, and drives more and more people into poverty, the materials required for cooking with imagination and creativity are obtaining an ever more phantasmatic status.[13] Actual alimentary changes, however, are of a lesser importance when it comes to culinary education, for, as I discussed in Chapter 1 in relation to the aesthetic politics of gastroporn, what is at stake is learning and adopting a logic of creative re-invention of the self and culture. Creativity as a way of distancing oneself from tradition is inextricably linked to the capacity to invent and re-invent oneself according to changing conditions and the shifting moods of the markets: creative adaptation as it has been often called by Greek psychologists (Mentinis, 2013).

Thus far I have deliberately limited my discussion to a national basis in order to unfold the rhetoric about cultural change within public and official discourse, whilst touching upon its culinary and alimentary dimensions. This is an insufficient level of analysis, however, for grasping Greek reality. The problem with the predominant discursive framing of Greek selfhood – exacerbated by Ramphos's portrayal of the Greeks – is that it singles out certain 'bad characteristics' in order to construct an average 'deficient' Greek self which is, practically speaking, non-existent. And what makes things worse yet still, is that it is this psychological portrait of the non-existent average 'Greek' that constitutes the basis for the government's decision making on economic and public policies (see Badiou, 2012). The discussion of the average 'deficient Greek' has an ideological function that serves to obfuscate that what is ultimately being carried out is the taming of the working class and the pacification of class struggle. It is this dimension I will now turn to.

Class war in the kitchen

The class character of culinary and dietary habits should not be understood in purely economic terms. More than this, it appears that even the bourgeois diagnosticians themselves approach it in cultural terms. For those diagnosticians, as well as their target audience, the East is foremost a geographical metaphor for the lower classes, for the proletariat – remember that the most destitute and exploited sectors of the proletariat in Greece are immigrants who come from the 'East'. Traditional, Eastern, (middle) Eastern-Greek cuisine is proletarian cuisine because it is repertoric, in the sense that its preparation follows tradition and habit. While it was once undoubtedly invested with lots of creativity, now one merely reproduces cooking conventions, executes recipes, albeit with no precision and no careful measurement. On the other hand, 'Western' gourmet cuisine is associated with the upper middle and higher strata of the population because it is creative. 'Western' dishes have no name prior to their subsequent naming which normally describes the main ingredients contained, they belong to no tradition, they simply do not exist until somebody brings them into being through the power of his/her own imagination and creativity; there are no pre-existent rules or routines to follow, one can mix ingredients as one sees fit, substitute one ingredient for another, play, experiment. These two different modes of cooking correspond to different modalities of selfhood and kinds of work: the first, to an Eastern, working class, irrational, immature, hetero-determined self who performs mainly manual work; the second, to a Westernised, civilised, autonomous, self-determined and creative self who generates ideas and performs immaterial labour.

A film that we can read as fusing together culinary and dietary habits with class and class antagonism, is *Dangerous Cooking* (2010, dir: Vasilis Tselemegos).[14] The film tells the story of two men, a renowned haute cuisine chef, Damoklis Dimou (Giorgos Horafas) and a sailor cook, Dimitris Savridis (Konstantinos Markoulakis), who both unwittingly fall in love and have a relationship with the same woman. The chef (interestingly, he is played by the same actor who played the passionate cook in *A Touch of Spice*), who can be considered the embodiment of the upper classes, has an aesthetic, erudite approach to cooking and attempts to charm the woman with his unique gourmet specialities; subsequently, she becomes the source of inspiration for his culinary experimentations and innovations, and upon sampling his dishes, she names them for inclusion in a gourmet cookbook he is writing. This process of naming is interesting in itself, as it indicates the lack of origin of these specialities: they are not rooted in tradition, they have no name, they are nothing less than the product of a creative mind, and obtain their names only by virtue of an equally creative act determined by visual and gustatory aesthetics. The chef, then, is a culinary artist, an autonomous person, one who throughout the film appears to have no family, no relatives and no friends. Rather, the people he interacts with are work partners, colleagues, acquaintances, who are all related to his job and career development as opposed to his personal life – indeed, even his lover is incorporated into his career development. On the other hand, the sailor cook has a more pragmatic approach to cooking. He charms the woman with his 'Eastern' naturalness, whilst the foods he cooks have pre-existing names, inasmuch as they are all derivative of the national cuisine. Moreover, his profession is a way of making a living rather than part of a career trajectory, or a way to achieve self-actualisation and/or publicity. Unlike the chef, he has a sister who works as a waitress in a neighbourhood cafe (family – lower class), and friends who are in no way connected to his job prospects and development. Furthermore, unlike the chef who cooks only with his own aesthetic standards in mind, he takes into consideration the desire of those that he cooks for, namely the co-sailors on the boat. He is not a fully independent and autonomous individual; he is hetero-determined, his self has 'Eastern' elements, he is a member of the lower classes, a person who is more attached to the past, as represented in *A Touch of Spice*, but yet not entirely so.

An interesting aspect of the film, which enables us to elucidate further how styles of cooking correspond to forms of selfhood and modes of work, involves a conversation between the chef and the cook towards the end of the film, upon realising that they have been sleeping with the same woman. The conversation is about cooking, and the chef is arguing in favour of molecular cuisine which he praises for its precision and exactness, that is, the quasi-scientific and rationalised way it is produced so as to take into account fine visual and gustatory aesthetic criteria. In molecular cuisine nothing can be left to chance, every single ingredient must be measured and considered in terms of its role in the final result, the chef explains. In other words, the type of work the chef praises is a product of creativity and imagination which is subsequently operationalised into a careful, disciplined and rationalised process. At the other extreme, the cook counterpoises that all of these aforementioned processes "kill the joy of cooking", the "beauty of the unexpected", the "magic of the contingent", "the accident, the mistake that might, nevertheless, produce a good result". Despite the fact that, at first glance, the discourse of the cook sounds like an exultation of creativity, thus signalling his agreement with the chef, it is not. What the cook praises, in actual fact, is not creativity per se, but the non-rationalised character of traditional cuisine, more specifically, the space that allows for an inattentive style of cooking, for mistakes – is this not what has been diagnosed as the fundamental problem of the Greek economy: its lack of proper planning and rationalisation?

The at first creative then rationalised, self-determined approach of the chef is contrasted with the almost 'magical' approach that plans little, and cares more for the 'joy' of doing than any mistakes that might occur in the process. The Greeks, according to prevailing discourses, are like the cook, and must become more like the chef. Towards the end of their conversation, referring to the life on the boat, the cook comments to the chef that "one cannot feed molecular cuisine to a hungry crowd of thirty sailors". The chef's reply is indicative of the type of selfhood he possesses: "it is not acceptable for the criterion of a chef to be based on the wild instincts of thirty savages", he replies. One's criteria, then, must be independent from the desires and needs of the proletarian 'savages', who, in turn, must be 'educated' and re-socialised; undergo a culinary rite of passage from savageness to civilised selfhood so that they learn how to succumb and conform to the upper classes' desires, tastes and projects –I'll return to this in the next section.

In the final scene of the film, things are put right between the chef and the cook. We see the chef relaxing in the terrace of a restaurant he has opened, after a long opening night which he mainly spent signing copies of his cookbook (I will come back to this also). The cook appears and places on the table a tray covered with a silver lid, which we are led to believe is food for the chef. A brief conversation then ensues, with the cook commenting jokingly that had he been the author of the cookbook, it would have been much spicier (an allusion to the details of his sex-life with the woman). The chef's reply is short and to the point: "To write a book you first have to learn how to write". We are once again brought back to the theme of the lack of 'education' of the lower classes. Lack of 'education' is partly a geographical issue (i.e. the 'old' Eastern Greece that is to be left behind), but is first and foremost a class issue (the uneducated proletarian must learn to conform and obey the knowledgeable elites). In this respect, it is indicative of a paternalistic obsession with 'education', and the particular meaning that the latter takes, that at the end of a TV interview with Stelios Ramphos, the journalist, recapitulating the teachings of the state's diagnostician, admonishes the audience: "So, let's find the way to education, that is, let's find the way to Europe" (2011, p. 74). Yet again, not to be European is to be seen to not have an 'education'.

Barbarian proletarians and the spirit of entrepreneurship

An important nodal point in the incitement of class struggle in Greece was the December 2008 ten-day-long contentious riots that followed the murder of a young student by a policeman in the centre of Athens. The riots unleashed an antagonism that was totally unexpected and virtually impossible to understand and explain within the prevailing frameworks and categories (Mentinis, 2010; Sotiris, 2010); they constituted a massive coming-together of sections of the working and lower middle classes, and express a strong dissatisfaction with economic conditions and the prevailing culture of individualism and indebtedness. Subsequent extreme austerity measures administered on the revolting 'barbarians' have functioned as an economic shock therapy aspiring to social peace and the taming of the working class. These measures have been accompanied by a rhetoric that holds indiscriminately everybody responsible for what has happened to the country and demands that austerity measures are stoically accepted. Ramphos's 'philosophical' rhetoric has contributed significantly to the promotion of the acceptance of the memorandums signed by the governments, and in directing attention to individual and cultural change as solutions to the Greek predicament:

> if we want to be creative people, creators of opportunities and horizons, who will put an end to the crisis with their dynamism, and not simply by saving money, we ought to combine carefully the extreme austerity measures of emergency with the anthropological parameter of the Greek problem.
>
> (2011, p. 91)

The problematic of class struggle and the need for pacification as a precondition for investments and the blossoming of innovations and entrepreneurship are indeed a common thematic in the discourse of members of the creative and entrepreneurial class. As Kalavros-Gousiou, founder and curator of TEDxAthens, explains:

> we have to give hope everywhere, especially to the active part of the community. There are many multimedia empires shooting pictures of Greece with riots, protests, fire, fights, blood, etc. We believe there is another part of Greece full of doers and people waiting for a chance to show their potential
>
> (2012, n.p.)

It is of course not clear why the protesters and rioters are seen to be the opposite of 'doers'. However, the young entrepreneur is wholly disinterested in these kinds of interrelations. What he really wants to communicate is a divided Greece: a country split between 'barbarian' proletarian unleashing 'destructive' forces on the one hand, and entrepreneurial creative passion on the other; a distinction between masses of protesting workers and the talented creative individuals, between unruly cooks and business-oriented chefs. Indeed, the last five years or so, entrepreneurship and investment in creativity has been identified by Greek and foreign politicians, economists and commentators as the only way Greece could get out of the crisis, and pave its way to development and prosperity (e.g. Politis, 2007; Dale, 2012; Rasmussen, 2012; Coster, 2013, Kotsios and Mitsios, 2013). As Forbes's Elmira Bayrasli (2012) puts it, entrepreneurship can be Greece's "modern Acropolis". Thus, proper education and training on investing, organisation, administration, human resource management, etc. (Poutzioris et al., 1997) as well as the awakening of the entrepreneurial spirit through the familiarisation of the Greeks with "success business stories, placing emphasis on ... the creative view of entrepreneurship" (Politis, 2007, n.p.) have been identified and actively promoted as essential for the emergence of the new generation of entrepreneurs and the creation of what the head of a start-up company calls the "Greek Zuckerbergs" (Tziralis, n.d., quoted in Coster, 2013, n.p.).

Let's return to *Dangerous Cooking*. The film – part of the 'education' of the Greeks into a new entrepreneurial mentality and the representation of class struggle as what prevents development and prosperity – registers a very interesting resolution of class antagonism. After the two men have realised they were sleeping with the same woman, their antagonism intensifies, and the chef invites the cook to his house for dinner in order to discuss the whole situation. As soon as the cook takes his place at the table and the chef brings the food, the cook is surprised to find the most traditional, working class food (often referred to as the 'national food'): 'bean soup in red sauce'. But this 'goodwill' gesture of embracing proletarian culture is soon shown to be nothing but a cynical ploy to trick the cook into withdrawing from the conflict over the woman. Eventually, the antagonism escalates further, and the two men decide to bring an end to it all by staging a final trial: they both must cook for the woman, each in his own signature style, the same traditional (Eastern) dish, *mouzaka*, and then have her decide which dish is the best and, consequently, which of the two men she will be with. Faced with such a task the woman refuses to try the food and leaves. The national body cannot be split on such a basis; both classes are required, what is important is simply who gets the upper hand. When the woman, fed up with what she calls their "childish fights", abandons them both, the two men engage in a process of dialogue. The aforementioned conversation concerning the different styles of cooking and their merits is part of this process.

Finally, the two men reach reconciliation and they are shown working in a restaurant together. The restaurant, in fact, belongs to the chef, where he offers a menu comprising of the new dishes included in his cookbook, whilst the cook is an employee in the chef's restaurant – albeit with a good position. The restaurant is thus neither a traditional Greek tavern nor a kebab shop. It is an haute cuisine, luxurious place for an upper class clientele who have both the taste to appreciate its newly created gourmet delicacies, and the money to afford its steep prices. One can also assume that the cook has adopted the chef's approach to cooking since he is now the head of the kitchen. In other words, the cook – acting as an exemplar of an obedient worker rewarded for his obedience with a post in the chef's kitchen – does nothing more than preparing, or at least supervising, the execution of the chef's recipes – what he maintains from his 'Eastern' self, from his 'traditionalness', is the aspect of executing things designed and planned by others, in this case the chef's recipes. The new components of his selfhood lie in the fact that, whereas in the past he prepared inattentively traditional recipes, allowing for mistakes and accidents, now he has learned how to prepare them with precision and careful measurements. The new obedient (and therefore rewarded) proletarian is not like the old one; he/she has been trained, 'educated' into neoliberal cuisine. The previous competition between the two members of antagonistic classes for the same national body (the woman), then, comes to an end only when the proletarian succumbs to the chef's project and conforms to his entrepreneurial projects. Creative entrepreneurship is therefore presented as the way to break from a past riven by antagonism and conflict, and embrace the harmonious future of class peace and modernisation. In the restaurant's opening night we see the cook, his sister and his friend (all working class people) working in a state of absolute panic in the kitchen, while the chef signs copies of his book and socialises with his affluent guests/customers. In the penultimate scene, in a moment of absolute docility, or as a way simply to express his gratefulness for his incorporation within the new deal, the cook tells the chef-entrepreneur that their former antagonism was "a stupid thing". That said, everybody must now occupy his/her place in the new Greek restaurant.

Culinary art therapy for melancholic Greeks

We need to return to the aforementioned joke that the cook made concerning his 'spicy' (and therefore Eastern/Oriental) past with the woman. What the cook actually expresses through this joke is his melancholy, his inability to let go of the lost object. Greeks are indeed diagnosed as melancholic, as existing in a state of never ending mourning, both for their ancient and Eastern past. The cook lost the woman, and he was compensated with employment; a subordinate position in the chef's restaurant. Unlike the cook, the chef is not melancholic; he still 'possesses' the woman – she was both the inspiration for the recipes and the one who gave the dishes their names. His creative and entrepreneurial capacities and skills have allowed him to bring the past into the present and future transforming it into something new: a cookbook with innovative gourmet recipes and a successful business. What the cook communicates through this joke, then, is both his melancholy and bitterness towards his exclusion from the process of writing the 'cookbook' that gives the restaurant its character – his education is inadequate, his knowledge insufficient for co-authoring a book, he can only learn how to follow it.

Critchley (2002) argues that humour is an anti-depressant that works by virtue of the ego finding itself ridiculous, and such humour is not depressing, but on the contrary gives us a sense of emancipation, consolation and childlike elevation. And he adds: "humour is an antidepressant that does not work by deadening the ego in some sort of Prozac-induced daze, but is rather a relation of self-knowledge ... it is a profoundly cognitive relation to oneself and the world" (p. 102). Now, even though the cook's joke is directed towards the chef – the implication being that he, the cook, had a better sex-life with the woman than the chef did – it does contain a knowledge of his position in the new conditions, and it is also liberating and soothing, in the sense that it allows him to confront his powerlessness in relation to the chef. In fact, we can say, following Billig's (2005) distinction, that, psychologically speaking, the joke allows the cook to relieve both his melancholy and powerlessness, but sociologically it functions in a conservative way, as it serves to avoid direct confrontation with the chef and thus perpetuates his subordinate position.

As was mentioned previously while the chef is relaxing in the garden armchair of the restaurant terrace, the cook appears and places on the table a dish covered by a silver food tray we are led to believe contains the chef's dinner. But after having made the joke, he lifts the lid revealing not food but *Kollyva* – a traditional cake, made of boiled wheat and sugar, which is offered in religious remembrance ceremonies following one's death. The cook, then, comments that a brief commemoration ceremony will help both of them to forget the woman for good. Can we take the cook's words seriously here? Is this commemoration ceremony the final act of escaping melancholy – and thus the final gesture of obedience to the new deal and acceptance of position in it? Or is it simply another indication of his continuing melancholy and experience of powerlessness – and thus a space for future resistance? It would be easier to guess if we knew the recipe of the cake.

Notes

1 This form of discourse concerning the country's position has been propagated by several intellectuals across the political spectrum. For example, the writer Nikos Kazatzakis, the painter Yannis Tsarouhis and the poet Odysseus Elytis have as early as the 1930s talked about Greece's meteoric position between the East and the West – often stating their preference for the cultural heritage of the East.

2 Constantinople was the capital of the Byzantine Empire. It is now the contemporary city of Istanbul.
3 Post-1453 Byzantium ceased to exist. The Greek speaking population (and contemporary Greece) were incorporated within the Ottoman Empire. The Turks brought and established a different cultural and administrative system allowing, however, the Greek speaking population to retain its language and religion.
4 Historically, and ever since Byzantium, the West has been viewed as a threat. Indeed, at times, it was considered a more dangerous threat than the Turkish one, a fact which is captured in the Greek saying: 'Better the Turkish turban than the mitre of the pope'. In today's crisis plagued Greece, the West (whatever this means) is once again seen by many as an enemy to the country's sovereignty.
5 One such episode was the violent expulsion of the Greek communities of Asia Minor by the Turks and the destruction of their cities in 1922. The migrants, who fled to Greece in their thousands, brought with them a distinct culture that bore a close affinity with the Turkish one. Some of the important cultural elements imported to Greece during this period which, ultimately, came to define popular culture were the culinary habits of Asia Minor and rebetico music – music that has its origins in Persia and, thus, structurally speaking, differs significantly from Western music. Other episodes that further strengthened the Western character of the country were, of course, the incorporation of Greece within the sphere of influence of the Western allies after the Second World War, the military junta's pro-Western propaganda in the late 1960/early 1970s, as well as the decision by the conservative government of Konstantinos in the 1970s to join the European Community.
6 The word 'Europe' is employed in Greece as if it is a unified place on the Western borders of the country, and more often than not is seen as synonymous with 'civilised life'. It is also a word that designates a mixture of individualism, an ethic of hard work, respect for the state, and a set of obedient behaviours, usually discussed with reference to specific patterns of organisation characteristic of northern countries (such as Germany, Sweden and Denmark).
7 This kind of split personality, or hybridity, is also attributed to the Western part of Turkey. It is indicative that, in his review of Orhan Pamuk's *Istanbul: Memories and the City* for *The Guardian*, David Mitchell describes Istanbul as the city "with West in its head but East in its soul" (endorsement of the English edition of Pamuk's book by Faber and Faber).
8 According to Eurostat, the number of Greeks in tertiary education in 2010 was higher than in countries like Austria, Sweden and Finland (see http://epp.eurostat.ec.europa.eu/statistics_explained/index.php/Tertiary_education_statistics), and, according to a European Commission Survey conducted in 2006, Greeks were more likely to speak a foreign language than, say, the Irish and the British (see http://ec.europa.eu/public_opinion/archives/ebs/ebs_243_en.pdf).
9 The Greek title is *Politiki Kouzina*, which is literally translated as 'Cuisine from Constantinople' (therefore, Eastern cuisine).
10 I mean neither to idealise tradition nor make a plea for a return to tradition. As Hobsbawm (1983) has shown, traditions are often invented, and

what passes for tradition often derives from the upper classes and only later becomes diffused within the population at large, or, in fact, originates in other countries. That said, to the extent that certain foods are widely considered within the Greek society as 'traditional', I employ 'tradition' as an analytical category that helps us elucidate culinary and alimentary transformations.
11 In order to understand better the rationale of this chapter the reader is advised to read Chapter 1 where the culinary metaphorics of the self are explained in more detail.
12 We should also mention here that the drowsiness that such food may cause, and the long break or nap that is often required to rejuvenate one's capacity for work, are rendered wholly unproductive and antithetical to the demands of capitalism, which requires agile, flexible, tireless bodies in constant move and capable of enduring long working hours.
13 In fact, in such conditions, a return to simple versions of traditional cuisine is increasingly the only way by which this strata can survive -- with a pan of bean soup in red sauce (the so called 'national food'), for example, a family of four can survive for two days at minimum cost; not quite the same as cooking salmon filets with avocado dressing.
14 The film is based on a book by Andreas Staikos (1998) with the same title published in English in 2000 with the title *Les Liaisons Culinaires* by Harvill Press.

5 From eating to starving
Gastrosexual men and anorectic women

Beyond the psychology of anorexia

Within psychology, approaches to anorexia tend to be dominated by a modernist, structuralist paradigm, whose logic dictates first locating the causes of pathology before subsequently developing psychotherapeutic interventions to deal with it (Botha, 2015). That is to say, biological, cognitive, socio-cultural, psycho-dynamic and systemic models strive to discover the underlying causes of anorexia, whether internally within the person or external in derivation, identify risk factors and clinical features, develop diagnostic criteria, design therapeutic techniques and assess treatment in terms of efficiency (see Kaye, 1999; Malson *et al.*, 2004; Botha, 2015). Within such a paradigm, anorexia is invariably conceptualised as an internalised, individualised clinical entity, which is to say that the person is thus pathologised as *having* anorexia, as *suffering* from a disease (Botha, 2015).

When it comes to pinpointing the 'causes' a number of 'internal' (individual) as well as 'external' (situational) aetiologies, ranging from childhood trauma, sexual abuse, intimate partner violence, alcoholism in the family, distorted body-image, extreme internalisation of socio-cultural standards of beauty and so on, have all been considered, and for that matter contested, as potential explanations for the onset of the problem (e.g. McGillicuddy and Maze, 1993; Coniglio, 1993; Jasper, 1993). In so doing, all have contributed, albeit to varying degrees, towards the pathologisation of the anorectic person, and their representation as a passive victim. Most importantly, what is ordinarily left out of such explanations – feminist approaches are an exception to this point – is the fact that anorexia is a condition which primarily affects women, and so what happens is that the gendered nature of anorexia is lost altogether amidst gender neutral aetiologies – cognitive approaches being the most obvious and clear example in this instance. Furthermore, despite the fact that many of the aforementioned factors can indeed play a factor in anorexia, their exaltation to the status of causal explanations is hugely problematic given that they are only weakly at best, if in fact at all, semantically connected with the actual problem itself. In other words, and this is something which is endemic to mainstream psychology as a whole, the same undifferentiated causes, say sexual abuse or violence within the family, are made to carry too much explanatory weight inasmuch as they are too readily employed to explain a veritable host of problems, ranging from eating disorders to hearing voices, without establishing clear and meaningful connections between the putative cause and the effect. That is to say, causal explanations are hardly causal, in the sense that they tend to merely link the concurrence of traumatic events and painful situations with anorexia, rather than, say, actually producing explanatory accounts.[1]

Beyond the disciplinary boundaries of psychology, feminist/cultural approaches have traditionally highlighted the absence of a proper cultural perspective in relation to anorexia, and have criticised the disembodiment and obfuscation of the female body that characterises both mainstream psychiatric and psychological explanations. Whereas some early cultural/feminist approaches established what now appears as a commonsensical relation between mediatic representations of the ideal female body and anorexia, thus, in turn, establishing a causal relationship between the two (e.g. Bruch, 1978; Brownmiller, 1984; Bordo, 1988), other accounts have now moved beyond this and via recourse to poststructuralist, Foucauldian theory have conceptualised anorexia in terms of the historical and discursive disciplinary practices that are involved in the production of the female body. Poststructuralist accounts pay close attention to the actual condition of women in patriarchal society and consumer capitalism, and see the female body as a site of contestation for a number of struggles (economic, political, gender, etc.) and inscribed with multiple discourses (e.g. Bordo, 1988; Grosz, 1994; Eckermann, 1997; Probyn, 2001, Mouda, 2011). In both cases, as Brain argues, anorexia emerges as a metaphor for women's oppression in a consumer culture (see Brain, 2002 for a review of the relevant literature).

Even though, as Brain (2002) correctly points out, there is a tendency within some feminist/cultural theories to substitute the dis-embodied self of psychiatry and psychology for a 'de-selfed body', which in itself is a passive subsidiary effect of gender power relations and social forces, it is undeniable that such theories do nonetheless set out to restore some kind of agency to the anorectic woman. The particular modalities of agency proffered by such approaches, however, vary considerably in scope and emphasis, with some theorists seeing the refusal of food as a way for women to deal with abject life conditions and experiences, and improve well-being (see for example, Brown, 1993; Zimberg, 1993; Recalcati, 2007), whilst others put forward a broader understanding of anorexia as a protest and form of resistance against the demands placed upon women in patriarchal societies.

A common thematic in cultural/feminist perspectives is to read anorexia as, ultimately, having an ambiguous message and a 'double meaning', in the sense that it denotes both an over-compliance with societal standards of femininity as well as a protest against these very same cultural demands that are placed upon women. Following this logic, Eckermann (1997) identifies a contradictory message inscribed on the emaciated body itself which while displaying a certain degree of docility, at the same time defies the prevailing health discourses of science and the authority of parents in an attempt for independent selfhood. In a similar vein, Benson (1997) argues that eating disorders need to be understood as "a complex response to the demands and constraints of contemporary femininity, involving both complicity with, and rebellion against, cultural norms around the gendered body" (p. 124). More certain in her reading, Grosz (1994) negates the dimension of docility and over-compliance, insisting, rather, that anorexia is a renunciation and parody of such cultural norms. Sharing a certain homology with Grosz's thesis, and writing from a feminist informed critical-psychological perspective, Fuller and Hook (2002) also see anorexia as a form of contestation and resistance – even when it risks being imbricated with privileged patriarchal forms – as it functions as a mimicking-cum-mockery of the masters' discourse of the female body. Generally speaking, it would be accurate to say that agency in anorexia is ordinarily understood in terms of control over one's body. As Lupton (1996) argues, anorexia is perhaps better understood as a technology of self-control and purification, in opposition to eating which represents a descent into chaos. Within such a formulation the denial of hunger becomes a "sign of triumph of the will over the body" (ibid., p. 135). Eckermann (1997) too stresses the aspect of control over one's body and argues, within a Foucauldian paradigm of the 'care of the self', that the person who starves uses her body to recreate herself as a 'work of art' conveying the message 'read my body'.

Even though feminist/cultural approaches place women centre-stage, discuss anorexia as an embodied experience and move away from simple causal explanations towards a broader cultural understanding, there nevertheless remain two important problems with direct relevance to our discussion in this chapter. The first of these is related to the absence of a theory exploring the relation between anorexia and contemporary culinary culture. Embodied or disembodied, feminist or otherwise, cultural or medical, theories of anorexia are characterised by an absence of any proper discussion pertaining to the prominence of food culture within contemporary societies. As such, to spew out food, to refuse nourishment, to close one's mouth are all normally understood either as the symptom of a pathology, or, in the case of feminist/cultural approaches, as a stratagem by which control and mastery of the body, and consequently resistance to the nexus of ideologies which seek to contain women, are expressed (e.g. Bordo, 1988; Lupton, 1996; Benson, 1997; Probyn, 2001). The second problem concerns the static and timid forms of protest and/or resistance that are articulated in relevant feminist literature. Indissolubly connected with this static understanding of resistance is what might be understood as the theoretical abandonment of the subject of anorexia in some kind of perennial limbo, as stuck within a perpetual loop of protest and resistance with no way out, no escape and no possible victory. Hesitant and insecure in the face of prefiguring alternative courses of action, such theorists relinquish the anorectic subject as prey to biological death, or allow its re-incorporation into the pathologising nexus of psychiatry and mainstream psychology, or both.

For the purposes of the present chapter, I will attempt to provide a 'food' specific account of anorexia through a discussion of the *gastrosexual* condition. Gastrosexuality as both a symbolic order and a structuring symbolic function is substantiated in the figure of the 'gastrosexual man' in the same way that Lacan's (1993) function of the Name-of-the-Father is performed by the individual father figure. Drawing on the Foucauldian concept of the *figure* as elaborated by May (2012), I discuss the gastrosexual man (a primarily male subject position) as involved in a complex set of culinary performatics which constitute women as prey and as 'edible' entities. The synchronicity of the figure of the gastrosexual man and anorexia allows us to embed the latter within food specific gender power relations. However, even though the concept of the figure may be adequate for discussing the positively valued dominance of the gastrosexual man, I argue that this would not be expedient in the case of anorexia. In order to avoid what is a largely static, and identitarian portrayal of the anorectic body/self, I have opted to abandon the term anorectic altogether and, instead, discuss anorexia as a *figuration* with reference to Braidotti's (2002) elaboration of the concept as the unfolding of a process of self/body transformation.

Psychologists working within the milieu of narrative therapy have identified the need to move beyond mainstream understandings of anorexia, and stressed the importance of externalising the problem, even though they too remain diffident in sketching out broader cultural narratives that can facilitate the process of re-authoring the anorectic experience (e.g. Fuller and Hook, 2002; Botha, 2015). Departing from structural explanations, as well as from food-free accounts, my intention in this chapter is to produce a food specific cultural narrative of anorexia – albeit, one among many possible other narratives – that allows us to produce a cross-mapping between gastrosexuality and anorexia, and see the latter as a complex dynamic flight from the former. As I do not intend to idealise anorexia and the suffering it causes, but rather explore its possibilities as an initial flight from the gastrosexual symbolic order, I conclude the chapter by discussing the impasse of the anorectic transformative process, before offering up an example that could constitute a starting point for fumbling around possible ways out of the problem.

Gastrosexual figures

Let us recall what we touched upon in Chapter 1, that is, Deleuze and Guattari's assertions in *A Thousand Plateaus* that within a machinic assemblage "what regulates the obligatory, necessary, or permitted intermingling of bodies is above all an alimentary regime and a sexual regime" (1987, p. 90). Keeping this in mind, it is important to also remember that in *The Use of Pleasure*, Foucault (1986) contrasted the ancient Greeks' preoccupation with controlling their diet with the modern obsession with sex, identifying a gradual shift from privileging food to an interest in sex in Modern Western societies (see also Taylor, 2010). In other words, what Foucault is proposing here is that it is now a sexual regime as opposed to a dietary regime that becomes the privileged site of moral restrictions, scientific inquiry and individuating reflexivity. I contend that this Foucauldian thesis is no longer valid. As Probyn (1999) argues, food is now a more important marker of subjectivity than sex. In her words: "bodies that eat connect us more explicitly with limits of class, gender and ethnicity that do copulating bodies" (p. 422). Although Probyn does grasp the re-emergence of the importance of food and its conflation with sex, it is Taylor's (2010) re-working of her observations that more explicitly expresses the contemporary intermingling of food and sex, or what we will call the conflation between the alimentary and the sexual regime: "it is not so much that food has replaced sex as our privileged form of self-constitution, or the other way around", writes Taylor, "but that gastronomy and eroticism have become intertwined" (ibid., p. 76). I name this vast, heterogeneous area where the sexual and the alimentary intertwine and conflate the *gastrosexual regime*; a symbolic order in which sex and food, the sexual and the alimentary intersect, conflate, stand in for each other (sex is food and food is sex) in a number of linear and hodgepodge ways and configurations. It is beyond the scope of this chapter to examine in sufficient detail the multiple ways in which gastrosexuality is formed and expressed in everyday culture, ranging from 'Viagra ice-creams for women' to cookbooks with semen-based recipes, not to mention from the food pornography of TV cooking programmes to dietary imperatives. In Chapter 2 I discussed an aspect of gastrosexuality in terms of the practice of placentophagy. In the present chapter I will focus mainly on the figure of the gastrosexual man, and the ways in which we can narratively connect it with anorexia.

As Foucault (1990) explains in *The History of Sexuality*, the formation of specific mechanisms of knowledge and power centring on sex in the eighteenth and nineteenth centuries gave rise to four figures as privileged objects of knowledge: the 'hysterical woman', the 'masturbating child', the 'perverse adult' and the 'Malthusian couple' – all of whom, apart from the last one, were negatively valued. Although Foucault does not define what a figure is exactly, he does make clear the indissoluble connection between these four figures and the preoccupation with sex during that historical juncture. What I propose here is that the passage to a gastrosexual condition implies that the figures that inhabit it will no longer be related solely to sex or food, but, rather, to both at the same time. For the purposes of the current chapter, I will focus on two of these subjective figures who are defined by their relation, albeit asymmetrically, to food/sex: the gastrosexual man, a masculine and positively valued subject position who substantiates the gastrosexual function, and the anorectic woman, a feminine and negatively valued subject position constructed by the psy and medical complexes. It is important to preface this discussion, however, with a brief but necessary digression on the concept of the figure, which I will do through recourse to Todd May's (2012) elaboration of the term. Doing so is essential as it will help us understand better the figure of the gastrosexual man and, more importantly yet still, will subsequently allow us to draw a crucial distinction between a figure and a figuration, the latter of which I claim to be more adequate in order to think of anorexia.

In exploring the concept of the figure in relation to Foucault's work, May (2012) first distinguishes it from Max Weber's 'ideal type'. This is because 'ideal types', given their status as mental constructs, cannot be found empirically anywhere in reality. Rather, they are themes that are more or less instantiated or expressed in particular individuals, and are the creation of someone analysing a situation from the outside. In contradistinction to ideal types figures are real (at least to some extent), inasmuch as they are created and defined by the environment in which they arise. "They are constructed", May argues, "through a series of practices that give rise to them by impinging upon individuals in particular ways" (ibid., p. 18). The hysterical woman, for instance, is labelled as such by practitioners. Similarly, we may add here, the gastrosexual man emerges within a food/sex oriented culture and is named as such by researchers and/or cultural intermediaries. In the same way, the anorectic woman is labelled as such by medical, psychiatric and psychological discourses and practices. Another distinction May draws between the Weberian and Foucauldian concepts is that, whereas ideal types are not normative, figures are essentially normative, as they do not just categorise, but also judge empirically. Thus, by being judged, "a figure becomes subject to certain practices of intervention, treatment, or recognition that reinforce or attempt to eliminate the characteristics associated with that figure" (ibid., p. 18). Again, one can see here how the characteristics associated with the figure of the gastrosexual man are culturally reinforced, while the anorectic woman becomes a subject of therapeutic intervention.

May goes onto explain, vis-à-vis Foucault, that neoliberalism allows one to participate in the economic sphere in any way he/she so fits or is fit to do, and in relation to the dictates of the market, thus bringing to life figures that are largely economic in character and defined by their relationship to the market. The two archetypal figures in this respect are the 'entrepreneur' – a figure whose identity is closely tied to calculation and investing – and the 'consumer' – a figure for whom buying/consuming forms an integral component of who one is. The figure of the entrepreneur is characterised by an active investment in the future: s/he makes plans, hierarchises preference, and calculates costs and risks, whilst continually striving towards maximising personal gains, whether material or cultural in nature; we might say that his/her engagement with the world is an active and even aggressive one. Furthermore, Foucault (2008) adds, neoliberalism encourages the individual to become personally responsible for its education, growth, development, acquisition of skills and valorisation of the 'self' in its capacity as capital. The individual thus emerges as an entrepreneur and an entrepreneur of oneself, being his/her own capital, his/her own producer and his/her own source of revenue (see also, Lazzarato, 2011;

May, 2012). At this point I want to think of the gastrosexual man as a particular substantiation of the figure of the entrepreneur, and the anorectic as a kind of anti-consumer.

The gastrosexual man

As aforementioned, gastrosexuality, as a particular manifestation of what we have called the name-of-the-chef, is first and foremost a function; a symbolic function, to be precise, which grants entitlements, rights and benefits, whilst simultaneously imposing rules, restrictions, interdictions (both dietary/alimentary and sexual/erotic), henceforth defining a domain of (subject) positions and propositions. It is this function that is constantly enacted by the figure of the gastrosexual man. The gastrosexual man makes culinary investments and expects sexual profits within a field where sex is understood in alimentary terms and food is eroticised and sexualised. He is involved actively in the culinary metaphorics of the self and, indeed, employs cooking as a means through which to perform the self.[2] The acquisition of 'culinary capital' (see Bell, 2002 cited in Ashley et al., 2004; Naccarato and Lebesco, 2012; De Solier, 2013) is an intrinsic part of the investment in oneself, and is indispensable to the performance and presentation of the self to others, including the process of seduction. In this sense, cooking can be said to be related to the 'care of the self', becoming a source of pleasure and entertainment in and of itself. As such, Ashley et al. (2004) argue, in relation to male celebrity television chefs from whom the figure of the gastrosexual man springs, the care invested in a meal is not a product of domestic labour, but, rather, of 'aestheticised leisure'.

The gastrosexual man thus enters the kitchen neither as a househusband nor a cook looking to share the burden and contribute to household chores – women, in fact, continue to perform most of the everyday cooking and kitchen chores (see Future Foundation, 2008) – but, rather, as a chef and for the strict purposes of colonising it as an open space of unbridled creative activity where new notions of masculinity can be performed. Installing his masculine gastrosexual authority in the kitchen thus infuses this space with a spirit of creativity, curiosity, adventure, the spectacular, exoticism, eroticism and seduction, which are counterpoised to what is constructed as feminine conservativism, sticking to tradition, routine, everydayness, motherhood, care and affection. "At our best", writes Colicchio (2011) in his foreword to Esquire's popular cookbook *Eat Like a Man*, "we bring that spirit of curiosity into the kitchen" (quoted in Kelly, 2015, p. 202). This notion of distance from women's ways of cooking is essential here. Referring to the cooking skills of the mother of a friend of his, Jamie Oliver boasts in the *Naked Chef*: "I've changed Mary's recipe to suit my taste, I'll probably get a slap for it but that's cooking and you can do what you like." Similarly, he is disapproving of both his mother-in-law's cooking competence, of whom he says that she "boils the hell out of spinach", and of his girlfriend's culinary skills: "my missus makes me fantastic mashed vegetables, beautifully seasoned and drizzled with olive oil, the only thing is that they are meant to be separate servings of boiled carrots and new potatoes" (all quoted in Hollows, 2003, p. 234). Devaluation of female cooking and the challenging of female authority, albeit even in an implicit way, are thus indispensable, I would argue, to the male gastrosexual position.

However, gastrosexuality, as I noted earlier, involves more than the mere involvement of men in cooking and the colonisation of the kitchen. It constitutes a whole repertoire that involves strategic thinking, agile skills of mesmerising and gaining control over one's mind, as well as maintaining a predatory stance the sole aim of which is seduction. As Iannolo writes in her discussion of cooking and sensuality:

> If I am preparing a meal for a lover, the intensity is magnified tenfold. Here is a man I wish to satiate in every way possible, and my act of seduction begins with his palate. I carefully choose the right flavor to heighten his sensual experience, balancing texture and flavor with deft hands to demonstrate my skills, and more importantly to excite his mind. I carefully watch his face as he tastes each dish, eager to see a reaction … [I]t is one long dance of foreplay.
> (2007, p. 245)

Incorporation of the 'feminine' ethos of care for others is often one of the tactics employed by the figure of the gastrosexual, which allows cooking to be presented as if it had somehow always been masculine, in turn, occluding conversation about persisting gendered inequalities in the home, workplace, and society more broadly (Kelly, 2015). Research seeking to explore the understanding and meaning of cooking between women and men suggests that, reflective of historically dominant ways of doing gender, women and men tend to construct cooking differently. Whereas women tend to describe cooking for others in relation to ideals of care that prioritise daily nourishment and affection, men's narratives frame cooking as an aestheticised leisure activity, that is, an activity whose main purpose is pleasure (Cairns *et al.*, 2010). Thus, if, as Probyn (1999) argues, the domain of cooking (and eating) is a privileged arena for the promotion of pleasure, sexuality and an individualised ethos of care, then we need to consider the ways in which this is especially the case in terms of the figure of the gastrosexual man, who, drenched in the codes of seduction and culinary performatics, targets the female body as a prey to be mesmerised, seized and 'eaten'. Preparing a meal, we could say, simulates hunting: food is the 'bait' used to capture the 'prey' which is then cooked in erotic heat and consumed. As Spencer Walker, the author of a cookbook entitled *Cook to Bang* writes on his webpage of the same name:

> Think of these lemon bars as the bait on a trap, a decoy if you will. Plant a seed with that sexy new coworker, naughty neighbor, or coffee shop acquaintance. Hand them a bar, allow them to experience the orgasmic indulgence in private and wait. Compliments and praise for your culinary prowess will surely follow. This is the part where you invite them over to your place for more of the same, but in a more intimate setting. Game, set and match!
>
> (Walker, 2015, n.p.)

Similarly, the gastrosexual man behind *Will Cook for Sex: A Guy's Guide to Cooking*, explains that "the first time I cooked for a woman I was young, the meal was marginal, and she was naïve to know any better. I got lucky" (Fino, 2005, p. 12). In both of these cookbooks one can discern the construction of a new feminine masculinity, one that differentiates itself from the idea of manliness as based upon "steroid enhanced muscles", for example, and instead performs an individualised repertoire of care through cooking in a tactical way, operating as a hook to lure women, to "keep a woman under one's spell", to "control the opposite sex's minds" (see Walker, 2010). The vocabulary found in these cookbooks is indicative of the interconnection and mutual substitutions between food and sex. For instance, in Walker's (2015) "charred octapussy salad" the actual food and the object of desire conflate to the point of becoming indistinguishable, as cooking coincides with 'banging'. It is within this context that anorexia, as an anti-consumerist stance, as an absolute refusal of food/sex, could be read as a radical departure from gastrosexuality. What the anorectic is refusing, is to derive an identity of prey from the gastrosexual symbolic order.

Anorectic figurations

Food is intimately involved in our dealing with others. From a very young age we celebrate and socialise with food; we also learn the meanings associated with eating, ranging from eating as a form of reward to not eating as either a form of punishment or act of rebellion. As Zimberg (1993) argues:

> We learn how to please when we are praised for being 'good little girls' when our plates have been cleaned, and are subsequently rewarded with desserts. We learn that saying no to food is a first and powerful way to rebel against our primary caretakers (most often the mother or a female mother substitute). We learn that being denied food is punishment for doing something wrong, and are soothed with food when we are hurt.
>
> (p. 138)

Mobilising Lacan's (1998) assertion that the anorectic 'eats nothing', Recalcati (2007) argues that anorexia is a refusal of the demand of the Other (Eat!), and thus can be said to constitute a subjectivising act that allows the person to establish a difference in respect to the maternal Other. In this section I want to depart from this kind of open reading towards a food specific understanding of anorexia. More specifically, instead of understanding the refusal to eat as a general expression of dissatisfaction, as Zimberg does, I wish to instead follow Recalcati and read anorexia as a refusal of the Other's demand to 'EAT!' This Other, however, is not the maternal Other, but a gastrosexual cultural condition. By closing shut one's mouth and rejecting food, the subject of anorexia chooses a form of deprivation, which allows her to reverse the relationship of dependency vis-à-vis the gastrosexual symbolic order, and its positioning and construction of the female body/self as edible.

In Margaret Atwood's (1992) *The Edible Woman*, Marian, the protagonist, whose anorexia has been read as a corporeal resistance to dominant forms of femininity and expectations related to women's behaviour (e.g. Brain, 1995; Lahikainen, 2007; Pei-Hsuan Hsieh, n.d.) begins her anorexic trajectory after watching Peter, her future husband, cutting and eating a steak. "The symbolism of meat-eating", as Midgley (1984) argues, is never neutral but one semantically linked to "eating life" (quoted in Adams, 2010, p. 181). Although Marian is hungry, a chain of associations and thoughts that run from her childhood to Peter's expectations of marriage and male 'accepted' violence make Marian realise that the steak is similar to herself and her body, as she is also an edible object, an 'edible woman'. It is instructive, in this regard, to also recall the scene we briefly discussed in Chapter 4. When the antagonism between the two cooks–lovers reaches its climax, the two men decide to bring an end to it all by staging a final trial: they cook the same dish for the woman, each in his own unique style, before then asking her to try them and decide which dish she prefers the best and, consequently, which of the two men she wishes to be with. In what is a properly anorectic gesture, when faced with the demands of two gastrosexual men to stabilise and control her desire and her becoming, she refuses to try the food, extinguishes her cigarette on the plate and abandons both of the men. She is not an anorectic, but we can read her action as a first step in initiating an anorectic trajectory.

Taking up feminist discussions of anorexia as a form of resistance, my intention here is to read anorexia as representing a line of flight from the oedipalised gastrosexual symbolic that constructs women as edible entities. In doing so, I opt to drop the term 'anorectic' as a largely pathologising category of identity, or even as a static figure of resistance, and instead discuss anorexia as a figuration, as a transformative unfolding, a becoming-minority, a becoming-woman as Braidotti (2002) argues vis-à-vis Deleuze. The subject of anorexia, then, is ultimately a dynamically changing subject; a subject existing in a movement of dis-identification from the neoliberal, phalogocentric gastrosexual symbolic, and thus involved in a process of transformation. Figurations, Braidotti (2002) argues, are "materialistic mappings of situated, or embedded and embodied, positions" (p.2), which allow us to account for one's location in space and time in terms of power as both restrictive and empowering, affirmative. On a critical level, she explains, figurations are a materially embodied account of one's power-relations, whereas at a creative level they "express the rate of change, transformation or affirmative deconstruction of the power one inhabits ... [they] materially embody stages of metamorphosis of a subject position towards all that the phalogocentric system does not want it to become" (p. 13). A figuration thus allows us to grasp anorexia as both a critique of gender power relations within the gastrosexual symbolic order, and a creative mode of dis-engagement and dis-identification, which serves to initiate a transformative movement of the self/body.

If man is, indeed, the standard bearer of law and logos, the 'dead heart of the system', as Braidotti (2002) argues, then we need to consider gastrosexuality as a particular way in which the law and logos are manifested through configurations of food/sex, in turn, defining a predatory and rapacious stance towards female becoming. An example from contemporary pornography may elucidate further the workings of the gastrosexual function at this junction. There is an obsession in porn movies today with a particular concluding scene that involves men ejaculating into the mouth of women. After having been sexually 'cannibalised' the woman waits patiently to be fed with the 'paternal milk', which she subsequently swallows whilst the camera zooms in on her mouth area. Discussing the eighteenth century advocacy of breast-feeding, Copjec (2015) argues that this was not meant to submit the child to the mother but, quite the contrary, to the social law. Even though Copjec focuses her analysis on the act of sucking, I would suggest in our particular case that it is expedient to direct our attention on what is actually consumed and its relation to the social law. Semen is no longer merely a sex related fluid destined for reproduction; rather, it is also constantly and insistently constituted and posited as a 'super-food' for women. Bodily fluids and secretions (urine, sperm, sweat, etc.), as Grosz (1994) argues, are detachable parts of the body which retain something of the cathexis and value of the person even when they are separated from it: "there is still something of the subject bound up with them … [they are] magically linked to the body" (p. 81). Extending Grosz's argument further, I would argue that the semen does not simply represent something excreting from the person, but, rather, is also something which is 'magically' connected to the gastrosexual symbolic order; it is the sedimentation of the gastrosexual condition.

In the same way that wine and bread are ritualistically transformed into the blood and body of Christ as a means of allowing the faithful to participate in holy grace and the Christian community, the aforementioned ritualistic pornographic scene constitutes semen as the holy communion that allows women to assimilate the spirit of gender power relations at this particular historical juncture. If the proper, clean, law-abiding and pure body is indissolubly connected to the abjection of body fluids and secretions, their keeping away from the alimentary tract (Kristeva, 1982), then we are now facing a situation in which the semen is constantly de-abjectised – something which is also reflected in the attempts to rationalise semen consumption by making reference to its nutritional value (high concentration of proteins, low calorie concentration, etc.), its beauty effects (effective moisturiser, good for teeth, etc.) and in terms of its putative culinary qualities as explained in *Natural Harvest*, a semen-based cookbook (Photenhouer, 2008). By incorporating and assimilating semen as the gastrosexual 'essence' the female body/self is bred in accordance with a gastrosexual male desire, and thus is stabilised and fixed as something to be cannibalised and consumed again and again.[3] Anorexia as a figuration allows the body to produce disjunctions and free certain organs/erogenous areas from their indexation to certain prerequisite functions now indissolubly connected with gastrosexuality. Having already indirectly altered the function of the reproductive system (amenorrhoea is a common symptom), the anorectic attempts to alter the oral and the anal tracts also (Grosz, 1994). The refusal to consume food, then, is the beginning of a corporeal and subjective process of dis-identification and metamorphosis.

The impasse of anorexia

If anorexia, as I have argued, begins as a flight away from gastrosexuality, it soon gets caught up in an impasse and loses its transformative force. On the one hand, the shrinking body structure (as well as amenorrhoea) of the subject of anorexia points towards a kind of enforced, extended childhood and a slippage into the pre-oedipal maternal semiotic *chora* where sexual difference no longer exists (see Kristeva, 1984). Grosz makes a similar point when she argues that "anorexia can, like a phantom limb, be a kind of mourning for a pre-oedipal (i.e. pre-castrated) body and a corporeal connection to the mother that women in patriarchy are required to abandon" (p. 40). On the other hand, in her absolute emaciation, the subject of anorexia looks as if she is forcing her way into the 'semiotic *chora*' of the 'mother earth', into death as it were; a kind of self-cannibalising structured around the suicidal declaration: 'I will eat myself before you eat me'. In both instances, the message she sends is that, if in the gastrosexual symbolic she is converted into an edible entity, then nothing will remain of her to be eaten. Hunger in this case is precisely the energy that allows transformation, allows the body/self to disappear. Unable to find a direction away from 'inexistence' anorexia thus arrives an impasse, and the figure of the anorectic emerges as that which is captured by a web of normative and pathologising discourses.

In examining further the argument pertaining to the wish to slide into the maternal semiotic *chora*, the impasse of anorexia becomes clearer yet still. As Kristeva (1984) explains, the semiotic *chora* is not a pure condition outside the symbolic as it were. Even though it is not governed by the law per se, it is nevertheless informed by socio-historical constraints. My contention is that these socio-historical elements are now operating along culinary lines. After all, what is the primary organ associated with the mother-baby connection if not the placenta, which, as I discussed in Chapter 2, is itself subjected to gastrosexual treatment even before it is expelled from the mother's body? The father who feeds his pregnant wife with 'chocolate digestives' hoping that these will endow the placenta with a certain 'taste' (see Baines, 2014) serves as an example of this sort of intervention into the semiotic *chora*, which, although it fails to impose a symbolic law on the internal rhythm of the maternal body, does nevertheless affect it.

However, returning to the womb is not even an option for the anorectic. What awaits outside the maternal body guarding against any return to it is the placentophagous chef or culinary expert performing his ritual in the kitchen. In other words, gastrosexuality has erected a culinary ritualistic barrier that prevents us from imagining a reconnection with the semiotic *chora* in these terms. The placenta is not even buried in the *chora* of the mother-earth. Instead, it has been gourmetised and eaten. So, what starts as an anorectic figuration, a flight, a transformative process ends up as a form of inactivity or inertia held in the dead space defined by the gastrosexual man and the placentophagous chef; a fundamentally alienating condition in which what the anorectic can demonstrate is nothing but a continuous sterile control over her desire.[4] What is the way out, then? What would allow what starts as a metamorphic flight to continue as such?

From this we must go back to Atwood's *The Edible Woman*. Marian, who is portrayed as having experienced an anorectic awakening, towards the end of the novel makes a cake, a 'cake-lady' as she calls it, that resembles herself but has an ideal female body, which she proceeds to eat with her lovers. This conclusion has been relatively controversial in feminist literature, as scholars dispute whether the 'cake-lady' symbolises Marian's final submission to the patriarchal world, a return to normalness – albeit with some degree of freedom – or whether the making and eating of the 'cake-lady' constitutes a ceremonial break from patriarchal demands, a symbolic cannibalistic act against 'perfection' that expresses the death of any desire to succumb to society's expectations (see Hobgood, 2002 for a review of the relevant literature). On the one hand, when serving Peter the cake, she explicitly rejects the manifold roles of a mother placed on her by virtue of her reproductive function, of a wife, of an underpaid worker and of an ideal manipulated woman. On the other hand, she seems to emancipate herself only through adopting male notions of autonomy and aspirational career success. Both readings, indeed, are very plausible. In fact, Atwood herself seems altogether unsure what to do with Marian.

What is important, however, whatever our interpretation of the end of the novel, is the fact that the solution is presented through a culinary metaphorics of the self. "As she coats the cake with sugar and colorful decoration", explains Pei-Hsuan Hsieh, "she is actually enacting her own experience of being dressed, having cosmetics put on her, and being coached to look more feminine and tempting to men" (n.d., p. 20). I would suggest, in keeping with what I discussed in Chapter 1, the making of the cake refers to something more than merely dressing and making oneself up: it is about the actual making of the self as 'beautiful', 'tasty' and as a 'sweet' product to be consumed, 'eaten'. She chooses all of the ingredients carefully, opting not to use things readily available in her house, but instead going to the supermarket to get fresh and new ingredients. Even though I see a kind of final form of docility in Marian's culinary metaphorics of the self, the important question raised at this point is whether we can employ a different kind of culinary performatics which do not mark an adaptation to neoliberal demands, but, on the contrary, produce disjunctions and disruptions, upheavals and ruptures that can allow the anorectic figuration to move beyond the present coordinates of self-starvation.

If gastrosexuality is indissolubly connected to the instrumental use of the kitchen by the gastrosexual man, that is, to the installation of his culinary authority and the concomitant devaluation of female cooking as being anachronistic, routine, traditional and unimaginative, then can we not also prefigure a way out of the limbo of anorexia along the lines of the re-colonisation of 'cooking'? This would not be about women going back to the kitchen and assuming traditional roles. Nor would it be a matter of merely re-negotiating in culinary terms new adaptive and adjustable female identities at the intersection of women's commitments as workers, mothers, wives, lovers and so on, as contemporary female TV celebrity cooks (the term chef being reserved for their male counterparts) seem to do (see Brownlie and Hewer, 2011). What I have in mind here, rather, is a creative repositioning vis-à-vis cooking that sets limits to and even reverses gastrosexuality – as well as the gastrosexuality of semen – so as to allow the female semiotic to explode into the male dominated gastrosexual symbolic, to overflow its boundaries with its uncontrollable excess.

Cecilia Westbrook, an MD/PhD student at the University of Wisconsin, Madison, appeared in several magazines when she explored the 'cooking' possibilities deriving from her making yogurt with her vaginal secretions. Apart from shedding light into the bacteriology behind her 'cooking' endeavour – as she explained that vaginal secretions contain a hefty amount of the enzyme lactobacillus essential in yogurt making – Westbrook also appeared to be aware of the broader consequences of her experimentation, making the allusion that women "should add more than love in their kitchen creations" (quoted in Simon, 2015, n.p.). Can we not read this "more than love" as an admonition for a kind of cooking that surpasses the thematic of female care and affection for others, and instead introduces the semiotic into culinary engagements? Whereas Westbrook's experiment was received with extreme caution by scientists who emphasised the potential dangers of vagina made yogurt (see Levine, 2015), cookbooks with sperm-based recipes for food and cocktails are now published and are widely available to buy even on Amazon (see Photenhouer, 2008, 2013) with no health warnings whatsoever. In Westbrook's case, it was microbiologists that expressed their disagreement with her culinary approach, arguing that vaginal secretions contain more than just lactobacilli and so the resulting yogurt will also contain other bacteria, some of which could be pathogenic (see Jay, 2015). If this is in fact the case, then one must ask why the same logic does not apply to oral sex? The point I am making here is that, whereas the consumption of male semen is ritualistically constituted in pornography and culinary literature as the 'essence' of the gastrosexual condition, female secretions, by way of contrast, are represented as 'abject', potential health hazards, and are excluded from the gastrosexual symbolic. It would appear to be possible, then, to think of another way out of the limbo of anorexia in these terms; a way that involves a total transformation of cooking and eating.

Notes

1 I do not mean to negate the importance of factors that have traditionally been associated with anorexia: melancholia, sexual abuse, etc. What I am suggesting is that we re-read these factors by contextualising them within a culinary metaphorics and in relation to gastrosexual power relations. For instance, Canetti (2000 [1960]) argues that the melancholic sees herself as being eaten, and this transformation into something which is eaten is the transformation that ends all flight. The melancholic thus refuses to eat because eating reminds her of this fact. Similarly, sexual abuse becomes important to anorexia because women become prey to the appetite of others.
2 It lies beyond the scope of this chapter to produce a genealogical account of the emergence of the figure of the gastrosexual man. The emergence of the discourse of entrepreneurship (of oneself), the boom in culinary culture, the accompanying emergence of the figure of the 'chef' as a culinary artist and an entrepreneur, changes in the concept of leisure, the increasing number of women seeking work outside the home, the increased numbers of men living alone and the delay of the age of marriage, broader changes in gender roles and division of labour, are all factors that have contributed to the transformation of the social perception of cooking

and the emergence of the gastrosexual man (Future Foundation, 2008; De Solier, 2013; Kelly, 2015). Although the term gastrosexual has been employed in order to account also for the gradual involvement of men in cooking in general (see Future Foundation, 2008), I employ the term in order to designate a particular relation to cooking as an aestheticised means for gaining certain rewards such as enjoyment, the display of skills and the presentation of self, and mainly as a form of charming and seducing sexual partners.

3 This idea of semen as a 'setting gel' is also found in Aristotle, who argues that it provides form not only for the growing fetus but also to the very formlessness of menstrual fluid itself, a function similar to that of 'rennet upon milk' (see Grosz, 1994).

4 Control over desire requires, however, further inquiry in terms of its capacity to keep the anorectic subject in its position. Lintott (2007) suggests we should approach anorexia in terms of the 'experience of the sublime' as discussed by Kant (1987 [1892]) in the *Critique of Judgement*. As she suggests, it is the vastness and power of hunger and the control over desire for food that causes the experience of the sublime in anorexia. In refusing food, the anorectic rejects the dominance of nature, of the physical self, and is thus able to contemplate objects immense in size and to resist the forces that threaten to destroy her (p. 64) such as hunger and starvation. It is this sense the awareness of power that keeps the subject entrapped within the limbo of the anorectic condition.

Conclusion
Towards a theory of anorectic cannibalism

Prune Nourry is a New York based French artist whose work aims to formulate a social critique framed in culinary/alimentary terms. However, even though her work successfully manages to creatively capture and depict the various intersections and conflations between food/culinary culture, science and capitalism, it is doubtful whether it constitutes a truly effective social critique. *The Archaeological Dinner* was one of Nourry's installations/performances presented in the Magda Danysz gallery in Shanghai in autumn 2013, and subsequently in Paris in the spring of 2014. Nourry invited guests to make use of archaeological research tools in order to dig through layers of food, and thus 'unearth' miniature male sculptures of ancient terracotta warriors. For this particular occasion, she created an original female sculpture which only one guest would discover in the final course, whereas all the rest would discover boys (Nourry, 2015). When considered in relation to Nourry's assertion on her website that this work was a critique of Chinese food traditions commonly used to increase the probability of having a baby boy, one would be justified in situating her work within a broader critique of the psychopolitical dimension of contemporary culinary and alimentary culture. The fact that terracotta warriors were actually found in a necropolis and were meant to serve as the emperor's guards allows us to claim that what the guests actually 'discovered' in their food was man as the standard bearer of law and logos, that is, the 'dead heart of the system' as Braidotti (2002) puts it. Consequently, the artist's insertion of a female miniature in the food of one of the guests could be read as a challenge analogous to the yogurt made of vaginal fluids discussed in Chapter 5; that is, as an attempt to interrupt a dimension of the gastrosexual symbolic.

After a more critical reflection on her work, however, it appears that Nourry's art, notwithstanding its assumed critical and feminist

Conclusion 97

perspective, is itself deeply ensnared by and entangled within contemporary culinary psychopolitics, which it both re-affirms and strengthens. In preparation for the performances in Shanghai and Paris, Nourry collaborated with renowned chefs – such as the Michelin starred Jean-François Piège in Paris – who, as explained on the artist's webpage, were charged with the task of 'following' the aforesaid Chinese food traditions (Nourry, 2015).[1] Nurry's choice of award-winning chefs, however, by no means corresponded purely with the culinary needs of the project. If the exercise was solely about 'following' these food traditions then it would have been more effective to recruit a native layperson who would almost certainly have a better knowledge of these practices. What the choice of a Michelin starred chef indicates is that the task of challenging tradition and inducing a separation from it actually required the function of the name-of-the-chef (see Chapters 1 and 2), thus meaning that her critical feminist deconstruction of patriarchal traditions was subsumed within a broader, neoliberal psychopolitics. After all, does her choice to represent her challenge to patriarchy through the use of a miniature female terracotta sculpture not also point to the subsumption of resistance into an equally military respect for the empire?

An earlier installation and performance by the same artist, again framed in culinary terms, was *The Sperm Bar*, which, as explained in the official press release from the funding institutions,[2] was inspired by the American sperm-bank industry. Nourry first invited men to symbolically donate their sperm by filling out an online donor application, before, in collaboration with top chef and mixologist Cristian Molina of the Michelin starred restaurant Rouge Tomate in New York, associating each individual trait with a particular ingredient/flavour. Each symbolic sperm donation, thus, produced a unique juice that reflected the donor's attributes (physical characteristics, intelligence, profession, ethnicity, religious views, etc.) – a brilliant example of what in Chapter 1 we designated as the 'culinary metaphorics of the self'. Nourry then took her project to Fifth Avenue, opposite the Metropolitan Museum of Art, on a food vendor's cart which had been renovated to resemble an aseptic sperm-bank centre. The role of the chef, here, was to prepare non-alcoholic cocktails corresponding to a selection of submissions from the donors available on the project's database, with visitors able to browse the donors' catalogue on iPads and select the ideal one for them based on the appeal of the recipe and the donors' characteristics (French Institute (FIAF), 2011).

Once again, my reading of Nourry's performance centres on the fact that its claim to question the commoditisation of human reproduction, the eugenics of baby-engineering, and the 'customer satisfaction' culture surrounding the sperm market is overshadowed by the reproduction of the gastrosexual condition – albeit a different aspect from the one discussed in Chapter 5 – through the symbolism of sperm consumption. Nourry's project, in fact, has nothing to do with baby-engineering, or at the most, is only minimally connected to it. The frivolity by which passers-by choose characteristics, and, indeed, their overall willingness and curiosity to participate in the project and consume the cocktail has very little to do with 'designer babies'; it is more about the metaphorics of 'swallowing one's sperm', 'tasting the other', feeling what the donor's characteristics taste like. In this respect, the chef acts as a high priest who performs the transubstantiation of fruits and flavours into 'sperm', and sanctions a joyous form of consumerist cannibalism; one based on 'taste' and preferences' and occurring 'out of curiosity', 'just for the fun of it'.[3]

In his writings, Marx at several points takes recourse to the 'vampire' metaphor in order to describe money, authorities (notaries, judges, bankers, etc.), the bourgeoisie and capital. Perhaps the most widely cited case is the one according to which "capital is dead labour which, vampire-like, lives only by sucking living labour, and lives the more, the more labour it sucks" (1990, p. 342). Exploring the meaning of this 'vampire motif' in Marx, Neocleous (2003) argues that, rather than employing it merely as a literary device inspired by gothic fiction, Marx wants to describe something real about the social world. Ruling out the possibility that the vampire is related to 'otherness' (women, Jews, slaves, etc.), Neocleous insists that to understand the meaning of the vampire metaphor it is important to situate it in the context of Marx's critique of political economy, and, in particular, the political economy of the dead, and his understanding of the dual character of both the commodity and labour. If Marx's distinction is between accumulated labour, that is, capital and labour per se, and what he calls 'living labour', then the growth of accumulated capital is the growth of the power of accumulated labour over living labour; it is not accumulated labour serving living labour as a means for new production but the other way around: living labour serves accumulated labour as a means for maintaining and multiplying its exchange-value. Now, if the distinction is between accumulated and living labour, then, as Neocleous argues, it makes sense to treat the former, capital, as 'dead labour'. Hence, the rule of the capitalist over the worker is nothing but the rule of dead labour over living labour; the latter appears merely as a means through which to realise objectified, dead labour, to penetrate it with an animating soul while losing its own soul in the process.

It seems to me that the vampire metaphor is no longer adequate for understanding neoliberal reality. Even though the parasitic relation it implies describes many aspects of life under capitalism, it is far from constituting the main pattern of the relationship between capital and labour. In contrast to the external relation between dead and living labour suggested by the vampire motif, cannibalism seems more apt for capturing the extended and hodgepodge nexus of the anthropophagic ingestion of otherness, even as it pertains to oneself as other. Benjamin's (2005) assertion that mankind's self-alienation has reached such a degree that it can experience its own destruction as an aesthetic pleasure of the first order conveys an ominous actuality: when asked by a journalist about *Hannibal*'s last meal before his comeuppance, Josè Andrès, the acclaimed chef who served as culinary consultant to the series – not to mention being beloved for his 'daring' and 'scientific' approach to cooking – replied succinctly: "Hannibal's perfect last meal would be a meat sashimi of every edible part of his own body that he would still be able to enjoy without pain" (quoted in Martinez, 2014, n.p.).

Even though, as Roy (2010) observes, vampirism has often been conflated with cannibalism qua an undisturbed ingestion of the other, they, in fact, constitute two very different forms of ingestion. Vampirism – and this seems to be the case also with Marx's use of the metaphor – implies a voracious appetite, for the sole purpose of self-reproduction, that is, the cloning of oneself. Indeed, Dracula does not suck blood so as to change, but, rather, to perpetuate himself as he is. In contradistinction to this, cannibalism, particularly in terms of how it has unfolded through today's culinary metaphorics, entails both a sense of occasion and a logic of expansion and change. Indeed, capital cannibalises not in order to re-produce itself, but in order to re-invent itself and transform. Similarly, to 'eat the other' – even when approached in strictly sexual terms and pertaining to white maleness as a state of incompleteness (hooks, 1992) – is not about a vampiric, parasitic self-perpetuation, but, rather, about the effect the ingestion of difference has on the self and the body in terms of broadening and expanding their experience. Furthermore, even though forms of 'anthropophagy', partaking in the other, ingesting him/her or being submitted to incorporation, can be said to be endemic to everyday interactions (Derrida, 1991), in neoliberalism 'anthropophagy' is transformed into a generalised instrumental form of cannibalism that objectifies and, in some cases, eliminates the other.

Despite the fact that the purpose of the present book has mainly been a diagnostic one, I want to devote these final words to prefiguring a course of action against neoliberal culinary psychopolitics through combining the coordinates of anorexia as a figuration of dis-identification from a neoliberal psychopolitics of food (see Chapter 5), and cannibalism in the original sense of the term. I believe that ethical action apropos food (Probyn, 2000), whether in its more conservative guises – such as Korsmeyer's (2012) 'ethical gourmandism' – or in terms of its more radical proposals – such as Naccarato and Lebesco's (2012) emphasis on 'competitive eating' and the culture of 'junk foodies' as a form of resistance to prevailing healthy eating ideologies, or Adams' (2010) feminist-vegetarianism as an attempt to deal with the sexual politics of meat eating – tend to follow a narrow agenda that insufficiently connects gastropsychopolitics to broader radical sociopolitical transformations. Gandhi's intertwinement of an approach to eating with political action can be of some inspiration here (see Roy, 2010).

Proposing 'anorexia' as a course of action requires maintaining its radical dis-identificatory characteristics while preventing the anorectic gesture from being subsumed into racist, nationalist, traditionalist politics, or simply as a form of dieting. Colonialism, as Roy (2010) explains in relation to India, invariably displayed a certain kind of anorectic stance towards natives, drawing a cordon sanitaire between the white bodies and the native practices of feeding and digestion – even though alimentary mingling of various kinds was actually unavoidable, and even sought out by the English when it suited their interests. We can also consider the more recent example of the overweight leader of the Flemish separatist party (N-VA), Bart de Wever, who at the height of the political crisis in Belgium in 2011 undertook a diet and managed to lose 60 kilos in eight months. De Wever's diet, which coincided with an accompanying 'power of change' campaign slogan, was a polysemous move that allowed him to demonstrate personal willpower against becoming 'hooked', alongside familiarising people with austerity measures – even though he was not included in the government. Most importantly, however, when viewed in terms of the problems between the Flemish-speaking Flanders in the north and the French-speaking Wallonia in the south, De Wever's was a gesture that conflated separatist politics with a distancing and abstaining from the consumption of food. Thus, to 'lose weight', De Wever suggested, one should adopt a simple stance: "no more French fries and Walloon Waffles" (see Robinson, 2012).[4,5]

In order to avoid pseudo-anorectic gestures it is essential to combine 'anorexia' with a cannibalistic politics. In the *Diario de Navegación* ('Navigation Log Books') of Columbus, we have the first European accounts of the ferocious Carib Indians who ruthlessly fought the Spaniards upon the latter's arrival to the continent. On Sunday 4th

November 1492, less than a month after Columbus's arrival, we read the following entry: "he learnt also that far from the place there were men with one eye and others with dogs muzzles, who ate human beings", and then again on 23rd November: "which they said was very large [the island of Haiti] and that on it lived people who had only one eye and others called cannibals, of whom they seemed to be very afraid" (quoted in Fernández Retamar, 1974, pp. 11–12). On 11th December, it is noted that *Caniba* refers in fact to the people of *El gran Can*, where the word 'cannibal' derived from. In Columbus's diaries the ferocious Cannibals are contrasted with the submissive and meek Arauacos; a binary representation of the natives we also encounter in Shakespeare's last play, *The Tempest*. Within this play, Caliban (Shakespeare's anagram for 'cannibal') and Ariel (probably a corruption of the name 'Arauaco') are two figures that are enslaved and robbed of their island by Prospero (the letters can be rearranged to spell out 'Oppressor'), a foreign conqueror. Unlike the submissive and obedient Ariel who binds himself to the master, Caliban is portrayed as brutish, vulgar and unconquered, displaying a sardonic and audacious rebelliousness against his master (see O'Toole, n.d.). This is a representation that reflects the epochal panic with the unruliness of the proletariat who preferred to risk the gallows than submit to the emerging conditions of wage-slavery (Federici, 2004). In this sense, 'anorectic cannibalism' emerges as both a radical actuation of a sectarian split from the alimentary and culinary psychopolitics, and as a radical unruliness against the neoliberal colonisation of life.

Notes

1 Nourry often recruits chefs for her performances. In *The Procreative Dinner*, another performance of hers, first presented in France in 2009, she brought together a renowned chef and a scientist to reflect on the idea of 'babies à la cart'.
2 The installation/performance was part of the French Institute Alliance Française's (FIAF), 2011 *Crossing the Line* festival in New York City in collaboration with the *Cultural Services of the French Embassy*.
3 The effectiveness of transubstantiation is captured in the words of a participant who admitted to having felt embarrassed to have consumed the cocktail:

> I went to the counter and they removed a vial of pink liquid from a cloud of dry ice, bringing to mind scenes of futuristic movies and images of aliens. As I began to sip the mocktail, I felt simultaneously embarrassed and intrigued. I could feel the scandalized crowd's judgment. For some inexplicable reason I felt the need to explain myself to every raised eyebrow in the crowd.
> (Marcum, n.d., n.p.)

4 Eventually, De Wever wrote a book together with journalist Carl Huybrechts entitled *Bart De Wever's Diet*, which mixes dieting tips and advice with discussion of Belgian politics.
5 In fact, even though it did contain elements of an anorectic gesture, De Wever's course of action was a pseudo-anorectic one and would be better approached as an extreme form of dieting, one which maintained its ideological consonance with prevailing conflations between alimentary imperatives, physical appearance and health. His diet was a carefully designed high-protein one, and he remained under constant medical attention throughout.

Bibliography

Adams, J. C. (2010) *The Sexual Politics of Meat: A Feminist-Vegetarian Critical Theory*, New York: Continuum.
Aguilera, I. (2008) 'Ingredientes Mapuche: Elementos para la Construcción de la Identidad Nacional', available at www.cidob.org/en/publications/publication_series/monographs/monographs/la_politica_de_lo_diverso_produccion_reconocimiento_o_apropiacion_de_lo_cultural.
Aguilera, I. (2009) 'Nuevos Productos Tradicionales: Entre las Politicas Agroalimentarias y la Multiculturalidad', available at http://sociologiadelaalimentacion.es/site/sites/default/files/Nuevos%20Productos%20Tradicionales%20FINAL.pdf.
Aguilera, I. (2012) 'El Ingrediente Mapuche: De la Cocina al Estado-Nación', *Unpublished Doctoral Thesis*, University of Barcelona.
Alimentación Sana (n.d.) 'Merkèn, no Solo un Sabroso Condimento', available at www.alimentacion-sana.org/PortalNuevo/actualizaciones/merken.htm.
Appadurai, A. (1981) 'Gastro-politics in Hindu South Asia', *American Ethnology*, 8(3): 494–511.
Appadurai, A. (1986) 'Introduction: Commodities and the Politics of Value', in Arjun Appadurai (ed.), *The Social Life of Things: Commodities in Cultural Perspectives* (pp. 3–63), New York: Cambridge University Press.
Appadurai, A. (1988) 'How to Make a National Cuisine: Cookbooks in Contemporary India', *Comparative Studies in Society and History*, 30: 3–24.
Aranda, L. (2012) 'Boragó: Filosofía Nativa en la Alta Cocina', available at www.dw.com/es/borag%C3%B3-filosof%C3%ADa-nativa-en-la-alta-cocina/a-16352971.
Ashley, B., Hollows, J., Jones, S. and Taylor, B. (2004) *Food and Cultural Studies*, London: Routledge.
A Touch of Spice (2003) dir. Tasos Boulmetis, Village Roadshow.
Atwood, M. (1992 [1969]) *The Edible Woman*, London: Virago.
Badiou, A. (2012) *The Rebirth of History*, London: Verso.
Baines, N. (2014) 'How I Ate My Wife's Placenta Raw in a Smoothie and Cooked in a Taco', available at www.theguardian.com/lifeandstyle/2014/apr/30/i-ate-wifes-placenta-smoothie-taco-afterbirth.

Bibliography

Barthes, R. (1972) *Mythologies*, London: Paladin.
Barthes, R. (1997 [1961]) 'Toward a Psychosociology of Contemporary Food Consumption', in Carol Counihan and Penny Van Esterik (eds.), *Food and Culture: A Reader* (pp. 20–27), New York: Routledge.
Bartolovich, C. (1998) 'Consumerism or the Late Logic of Cannibalism', in Francis Barker, Peter Hulme and Margaret Iverson (eds.), *Cannibalism and the Colonial World* (pp. 202–237), Cambridge: Cambridge University Press.
Bayrasli, E. (2012) 'Building the Modern Acropolis: Greek Entrepreneurs', available at www.forbes.com/sites/elmirabayrasli/2012/02/27/building-the-modern-acropolis-greek-entrepreneurs/.
Bengoa, J. (2000) *La Historia del Pueblo Mapuche: Siglo XIX Y XX*, Santiago de Chile: LOM.
Benjamin, W. (2005 [1936]) 'The Work of Art in the Age of Mechanical Reproduction', available at https://www.marxists.org/reference/subject/philosophy/works/ge/benjamin.htm.
Benson, S. (1997) 'The Body, Health and Eating Disorders', in Kathryn Woodward (ed.), *Identity and Difference* (pp. 121–181), London: Sage.
Billig, M. (2005) *Laughter and Ridicule: Towards a Social Critique of Humour*, London: Sage Publications.
Binkley, S. (2006) 'Lifestyle Print Culture and Mediation of Everyday Life: From Dispersing Images to Caring Texts', in David Bell and Joanne Hollows (eds.), *Historicizing Lifestyle: Mediating Taste, Consumption and Identity from 1900s to 1970s* (pp. 108–130), Farnham: Ashgate Publishing.
Blue, A. (1992) 'The Rise of the Greek Professional Ethnopsychiatry', in Atwood D. Gaines (ed.), *Ethnopsychiatry: The Cultural Construction of Professional and Folk Psychiatries* (pp. 327–354), Albany, NY: State University of New York Press.
Boltanski, L. and Chiapello, E. (2005) *The New Spirit of Capitalism*, London: Verso.
Bordo, S. (1988) 'Anorexia Nervosa: Psychopathology as the Crystallization of Culture', in Irene Diamond and Lee Quinby (eds.), *Feminism and Foucault: Reflections on Resistance* (pp. 226–250), Boston: Northeastern University Press.
Botha, D. (2015) 'Anorexia Nervosa: A Fresh Perspective', *Theory & Psychology*, available at http://tap.sagepub.com/content/early/2015/01/17/0959354314566490.abstract.
Bourdieu, P. (1984) *Distinction: A Social Critique of the Judgment of Taste*, London: Routledge & Kegan Paul.
Brady, E. (2012) 'Smells, Tastes, and Everyday Aesthetics', in David M. Kaplan (ed.), *The Philosophy of Food* (pp. 69–86), Los Angeles: University of California Press.
Braidotti, R. (2002) *Metamorphoses: Towards a Materialist Theory of Becoming*, Cambridge: Polity.
Brain, J. (2002) 'Unsettling Body-Image: Anorexic Body Narratives and the Materialization of the Body-Imaginary', *Feminist Theory*, 3(2): 151–168.

Brain, T. (1995) 'Figuring Anorexia: Margaret Atwood's *The Edible Woman*', *Literature, Interpretation, Theory*, 6(3–4): 299–311.
Brenner, N. and Theodore, N. (2002) 'Cities and the Geographies of "Actually Existing Neoliberalism"', *Antipode*, 34(3): 349–379.
Brenner, N. and Theodore, N. (2005) 'Neoliberalism and the Urban Condition', *City*, 9(1): 101–107.
Briones, C. (2002) 'Mestisaje y Blanqueamiento como Coordenadas de Aboriginalidad y Nación en Argentina', *RUNA: Archivo para las Ciencias del Hombre*, XXIII: 61–88.
Brown, C. (1993) 'The Continuum: Anorexia, Bulimia, and Weight Preoccupation', in Catrina Brown and Karin Jasper (eds.), *Consuming Passions: Feminist Approaches to Weight Preoccupation and Eating Disorders* (pp. 53–68), Toronto: Second Story Press.
Brownlie, D. and Hewer, P. (2011) '(Re)covering the Spectacular Domestic: Culinary Cultures, the Feminine Mundane, and Brand Nigella', *Advertising & Society Review*, available at http://muse.jhu.edu/login?auth=0&type= summary&url=/journals/advertising_and_society_review/v012/12.2.brownlie.html.
Brownlie, D., Hewer, P. and Horne, S. (2005) 'Culinary Tourism: An Exploratory Reading of Contemporary Representations of Cooking', *Consumption, Markets and Culture*, 8(1): 7–26.
Brownmiller, S. (1984) *Femininity*, New York: Simon and Schuster.
Bruch, H. (1978) *The Golden Cage: The Enigma of Anorexia Nervosa*, Cambridge, MA: Harvard University Press.
Bull, S. (2013) '"I'd Highly Suggest it to Any Pregnant Woman": January Jones Says Consuming her Placenta Helped her Beat Baby Blues', *Daily Mail online*, available at www.dailymail.co.uk/tvshowbiz/article-2285898/January-Jones-says-consuming-placenta-helped-beat-baby-blues.html.
Bywater, M. (2001) 'How to be a Domestic Porn Star', *The Independent*, available at www.independent.co.uk/news/media/how-to-be-a-domestic-porn-star-9211560.html.
Cable, S. (2011) 'Embarrassingly Wet: Jamie Oliver's Verdict on British Youth', available at www.dailymail.co.uk/tvshowbiz/article-1356599/Jamie-Oliver-attacks-British-youth-embarrassingly-wet.html.
Cairns, K., Johnston, J. and Baumann, S. (2010) 'Caring About Food: Doing Gender in the Foodie Kitchen', *Gender and Society*, 24(5): 591–615.
Canetti, E. (2000 [1960]) *Crowds and Power*, New York: Continuum.
Chaney, D. C. (1996) *Lifestyles*, New York: Routledge.
Chaney, D. C. (2002) *Cultural Change and Everyday Life*, Basingstoke: Palgrave.
Channel 4 (1998) 'TV Dinners', *Channel 4*, series 3, episode 5, available at www.channel4.com/programmes/tv-dinners/on-demand/25046-005.
Chevalier, M. J. and Sánchez Bain, A. (2003) *The Hot and the Cold: The Ills of Humans and Maize in Native Mexico*, Toronto: University of Toronto Press.
Claiborne, C. (1985) 'Young Chefs: From Anthropology to Haute Cuisine', available at www.nytimes.com/1985/10/02/garden/young-chefs-from-anthropology-to-haute-cuisine.html.

Coniglio, C. (1993) 'Making Connections: Family Alcoholism and the Development of Eating Problems', in Catrina Brown and Karin Jasper (eds.), *Consuming Passions: Feminist Approaches to Weight Preoccupation and Eating Disorders* (pp. 235–250), Toronto: Second Story Press.

Copjec, J. (2015) *Read My Desire: Lacan Against the Historicists*, London: Verso.

Coster, H. (2013) 'Could Entrepreneurship Jump-start Greece's Economy?', available at www.ekathimerini.com/4dcgi/_w_articles_wsite2_1_31/10/2013_525533.

Critchley, S. (2002), *On Humour*, London: Routledge.

Crow, J. (2013) *The Mapuche in Modern Chile: A Cultural History*, Gainesville: University Press of Florida.

Cusack, I. (2000) 'African Cuisines: Recipes for Nation-building?' *Journal of African Cultural Studies*, 13(2): 207–225.

Cwiertka, K. J. (2006) *Modern Japanese Cuisine: Food, Power, and National Identity*, London: Reaktion Books.

Dale, D. (2012) 'Greek Economic Crisis: Entrepreneurs Face Olympian Hurdles', available at www.thestar.com/news/world/2012/07/04/greek_economic_crisis_entrepreneurs_face_olympian_hurdles.html.

Dangerous Cooking (2010), dir. Vasilis Tselemegos, Odeon.

Dardot, P. and Laval, C. (2013) *The New Way of the World: On Neoliberal Society*, London: Verso.

Davidson, R. J. (1983) 'La Sombra de la Vida: La Placenta en el Mundo Andino', *Bulletin de l'Institut Français d'Etudes Andines*, available at www.ifeanet.org/publicaciones/boletines/12(3–4)/69.pdf.

Davidson, R. J. (1985) 'The Shadow of Life: Psychosocial Explanations for Placenta Rituals', *Culture, Medicine and Psychiatry*, 9(1): 75–92.

Davies, C. E. (2003) 'Language and American "Good Taste": Martha Stewart as Mass-media Role Model', in Jean Aitchson and Diana M. Lewis (eds.), *New Media Language* (pp. 146–156), London: Routledge.

Davis, B. (2013) *9.5 Theses on Art and Class*, Chicago: Haymarket Books.

Davis, S. (2015) 'Pastry Chef Annabel Lecter Will Turn Your Nightmares into Cake', *Vice*, available at www.vice.com/read/pastry-chef-annabel-lecter-will-turn-your-nightmares-into-cake-309.

Dean, N. (2010) 'Death by Spin: Piñera Orchestrates "Ultimate Pacification in Araucania"', *Mapuche International Link*, available at http://mapuche-nation.org/english/html/articles/art-21.htm.

Deleuze, G. and Guattari, F. (1987) *A Thousand Plateaus: Capitalism and Schizophrenia*, Minneapolis: University of Minnesota Press.

Derrida, J. (1991) '"Eating Well" or the Calculation of the Subject: An Interview with Jacques Derrida', in Eduardo Cadava, Jean-Luc Nancy and Peter Connor (eds.), *Who Comes After the Subject* (pp. 96–119), London: Routledge.

De Solier, I. (2013) *Food and the Self: Consumption, Production and Material Culture*, London: Bloomsbury.

Bibliography

De Vos, J. (2012) *Psychologisation in Times of Neoliberalism*, London: Routledge.
Dilts, A. (2011) 'From "Entrepreneur of the Self" to "Care of the Self": Neo-liberal Governmentality and Foucault's Ethics', *Foucault Studies*, 12: 130–146.
Eckermann, L. (1997) 'Foucault, Embodiment, and Gendered Subjectivities: The Case of Voluntary Self-Starvation', available at www.academyanalyticarts.org/eckermann.htm.
Educar Chile (2013) 'En este Colegio la Cultura Mapuche está Presente en Todas las Materias', available at www.educarchile.cl/ech/pro/app/detalle?id=195732.
Elias, N. (2000 [1939]) *The Civilising Process: Sociogenetic and Psychogenetic Investigations*, revised edition, Oxford: Blackwell.
Elyada, O. (n.d.) 'The Raw and the Cooked: Claude Lévi-Strauss and the Hidden Structures of Myth', available at http://art-gallery.haifa.ac.il/raw-cooked/pdf/elyada-e.pdf.
Fahim, J. (2012) *Beyond Cravings: Gender and Class Desires in Chocolate Marketing*, Saarbrücken: Lap Lambert Academic Publishing.
Farrell, E. (2000) *Lost for Words: The Psychoanalysis of Anorexia and Bulimia*, New York: Other Press.
Featherstone, M. (1991a) 'The Body in Consumer Culture', in Mike Featherstone, Mike Hepworth and Bryan Turner (eds.), *The Body: Social Process and Cultural Theory* (pp. 170–196), London: Sage.
Featherstone, M. (1991b) *Consumer Culture and Postmodernism*, London: Sage.
Federici, S. (2004) *Caliban and The Witch: Women, the Body and Primitive Accumulation*, New York: Autonomedia.
Fernández Juárez, G. (2002) *Aymaras de Bolivia: Entre la Tradición y el Cambio Cultural*, Quito, Ecuador: Ediciones Abya-Yala.
Fernández Retamar, R. (1974) 'Caliban: "Notes Towards a Discussion of Culture in Our America"', *The Massachusetts Review*, 15(1): 7–72.
Fino, R. (2005) *Will Cook for Sex: A Guy's Guide to Cooking*, Las Vegas: Stephens Press.
Floyd, J. (2004) 'Coming Out of the Kitchen: Texts, Contexts and Debates', *Cultural Geographies*, 10: 61–73.
Food and Agriculture Organisation (FAO) (2011) 'Recetario Internacional De Productos del Mar', available at www.subpesca.cl/publicaciones/606/articles-79722_recurso_1.pdf.
Food and Agriculture Organisation (FAO) (2014) 'Recetario Internacional De la Quinua: *Tradición y Vanguardia*, available at www.fao.org/docrep/019/i3525s/i3525s.pdf.
Food Empowerment Project (2015) 'Child Labour and Slavery in the Chocolate Industry', available at www.foodispower.org/slavery-chocolate/.
Foucault, M. (1984) 'Of Other Spaces: Utopias and Hererotopias', *Architecture/Movement/Continuitè*, available at http://web.mit.edu/allanmc/www/foucault1.pdf.

Bibliography

Foucault, M. (1986) *The Use of Pleasure*, New York: Vintage Books.

Foucault, M. (1990 [1976]) *The Will to Knowledge (The History of Sexuality Vol. 1)*, London: Penguin Books.

Foucault, M. (1993) 'About the Beginning of the Hermeneutics of the Self' (Transcription of two lectures in Dartmouth on 17 and 24 November 1980), ed. Mark Blasius, in *Political Theory*, 21(2): 198–227.

Foucault, M. (2008) *The Birth of Biopolitics: Lectures at the Collège de France, 1978–1979*, London: Palgrave Macmillan.

French Institute (FIAF) (2011) 'Crossing the Line: The Sperm Bar', available at www.fiaf.org/crossingtheline/2011/documents/CTL11-PR-Prune-Nourry.pdf.

Fuller, S. and Hook, D. (2002) 'Rewriting the Body, Reauthoring the Expert: Reading the Anorexic Body', in Derek Hook and Gillian Eagle (eds.), *Psychopathology and Social Prejudice* (pp. 110–123), Cape Town: University of Cape Town Press.

Future Foundation (2008) 'The Emergence of the Gastrosexual', available at www.theadnostic.com/lauren/EmergenceoftheGastrosexual.pdf.

Garval, M. (2007) 'Alexis Soyer and the Rise of the Celebrity Chef', *Romantic Circle Praxis*, available at www.rc.umd.edu/praxis/gastronomy/garval/garval_essay.html.

Gatica, L. (2008) 'Mapuche Chef rescata su Cocina', *El Mercurio*, available at www.mapuche.info/news/merc080414.html.

Gestalt Foundation – Athens (2011) The Creative Adaptations of a Society in Crisis. 13th four-day workshop on Gestalt Psychotherapy, available at www.gestaltfoundation.gr/page.php?id=48.

Gestalt Foundation – Athens (2012) Thinking, Feeling, Observing, Experimenting, Growing: Experience and Process in Gestalt Therapy. 14th four-day workshop on Gestalt Psychotherapy, available at www.gestalt foundation.gr/page.php?id=49.

Gibson, J. (1998) 'Watchdog Finds Placenta Dinner in Bad Taste', *The Independent*, available at www.independent.co.uk/news/watchdog-finds-placenta-dinner-in-bad-taste-1156466.html.

Giddens, A. (1990) *The Consequences of Modernity*, Stanford: Stanford University Press.

Gigante, D. (2007) 'Romantic Gastronomy: An Introduction', *Romantic Circle Praxis*, available at www.rc.umd.edu/praxis/gastronomy/gigante/gigante_essay.html#1.

Gillespie, C. H. (1994) 'Gastrosophy and *Nouvelle Cuisine*: Entrepreneurial Fashion and Fiction', *British Food Journal*, 96(10): 19–23.

Goldhill, O. (2013) 'Jamie Oliver's Soapbox – the Opinions of the Outspoken Chef', available at www.telegraph.co.uk/news/celebritynews/10269166/Jamie-Olivers-soapbox-the-opinions-of-the-outspoken-chef.html.

Goody, J. (1982) *Cooking, Cuisine and Class: A Study in Comparative Sociology*, Cambridge: Cambridge University Press.

Gray, E. (2015) 'Necrophagy at the Lynching Block', *on the visceral*, available at http://onthevisceral.tumblr.com/.

Bibliography 109

Green, S. (2014) 'What Do Steve Jobs, Richard Branson, and Jamie Oliver Have in Common?', available at www.thegeniuscompany.co/genius-business-blog/what-do-steve-jobs-richard-branson-and-jamie-oliver-have-in-common-by-soleira-green.

Grosz, E. (1994) *Volatile Bodies: Towards a Corporeal Feminism*, Indianapolis: Indiana University Press.

Guy, L. (2005) 'When Champagne Became French: Wine and the Making of a National Identity', *The American Historical Review*, 110(1): 232–233.

Hale, C. R. (2002) 'Does Multiculturalism Menace? Governance, Cultural Rights and the Politics of Identity in Guatemala', *Journal of Latin American Studies*, 34: 485–524.

Hale, C. R. (2004) 'Rethinking Indigenous Politics in the Era of the "Indio Permitido"', *NACLA Report of the Americas*, 38(2): 17–27.

Hamann, T. (2009) 'Neoliberalism, Governmentality and Ethics', *Foucault Studies*, 6: 37–59.

Harper's Magazine (1999) 'Save Some Womb for Dessert' (television transcript), *Harper's Magazine*, available at http://harpers.org/archive/1999/02/save-some-womb-for-dessert/.

Harpur, P. (2009 [2002]) *The Philosophers' Secret Fire: A History of the Imagination*, Glastonbury: The Squeeze Press.

Harvey, D. (2007) *A Brief History of Neoliberalism*, Oxford: Oxford University Press.

Haughney, D. (2005) 'Sustainable Development or Sustained Conflict? Logging Companies, Neoliberal Policies and Mapuche Communities', in Silvia Nagy-Zekmi and Fernando I. Leiva (eds.), *Democracy in Chile: The Legacy of September 11, 1971* (pp. 89–98), Brighton: Sussex Academic Press.

Hebdige, D. (1979) *Subculture: The Meaning of Style*, London: Methuen and Co.

Helstosky, C. (2010) 'Recipe for the Nation: Reading Italian History through La Scienza in Cusina and La Cusina Futurista', *Food & Foodways*, II(2–3): 113–140.

Hobgood, J. (2002) 'Anti-edibles: Capitalism and Schizophrenia in Margaret Atwood's *The Edible Woman*', *Style*, 36(1): 146–169.

Hobsbawm, E. (1983) 'Introduction: Inventing Traditions', in Eric Hobsbawm and Terence Ranger (eds.), *The Invention of Tradition* (pp. 1–14), Cambridge: Cambridge University Press.

Hollows, J. (2003) 'Oliver's Twist: Leisure, Labour and Domestic Masculinity in The Naked Chef', *International Journal of Cultural Studies*, 6(2): 229–248.

Hollows, J. and Jones, S. (2010) '"At Least He's Doing Something": Moral Entrepreneurship and Individual Responsibility in Jamie's *Ministry of Food*', *European Journal of Cultural Studies*, 13(3): 307–322.

Homer, S. (2005) *Jacques Lacan*, New York: Routledge.

hooks, b. (1992) *Black Looks: Race and Representation*, Boston: South End Press.

Iannolo, L. J. (2007) 'Food and Sensuality: A Perfect Pairing', in Fritz Allhoff and Dave Monroe (eds.), *Food and Philosophy: Eat, Drink and Be Merry* (pp. 239–249), Malden, MA: Blackwell.

Bibliography

Iggers, J. (2007) 'Who Needs a Critic? The Standard of Taste and the Power of Branding', in Fritz Allhoff and Dave Monroe (eds.), *Food and Philosophy: Eat, Drink and Be Merry* (pp. 88–101), Malden, MA: Blackwell.

Ivanovic Willumsen, C. (2004) 'Nueva Cocina Chilena: Culinaria e Identidad', Doctoral Thesis, available at http://repositorio.uchile.cl/bitstream/handle/2250/115072/Catalina%20Ivanovic%20Willumsen.pdf?sequence=1&isAllowed=y.

Jameson, F. (1991) *Postmodernism, or, the Cultural Logic of Late Capitalism*, Durham, NC: Duke University Press.

Jasper, K. (1993) 'Out From Under Body-Image Disparagement', in Catrina Brown and Karin Jasper (eds.), *Consuming Passions: Feminist Approaches to Weight Preoccupation and Eating Disorders* (pp. 195–218), Toronto: Second Story Press.

Jay, J. (2015) 'How to Make Breakfast with your Vagina', available at http://motherboard.vice.com/read/how-to-make-breakfast-with-your-vagina.

Jay, M. (1992) '"The Aesthetic Ideology" as Ideology: Or, What Does it Mean to Aestheticize Politics?', *Cultural Critique*, 21 (Spring): 41–61.

Kalavros-Gousiou, D. (2012) Bringing Greece into the future (interview), available at www.hellenext.org/reinventing-greece/2012/01/bringing-greece-into-the-future-with-tedxathens/.

Kant, E. (1987 [1892]) *Critique of Judgement*, trans. Werner Pluhar, Indianapolis: Heckett Publishing.

Kaye, J. D. (1999) 'Towards a Non-regulative Praxis', in Ian Parker (ed.), *Deconstructing Psychotherapy* (pp. 19–38), London: Sage.

Kearney, R. (2005) *The Wake of Imagination*, London: Routledge.

Kelly, R. C. (2015) 'Cooking Without Women: The Rhetoric of the New Culinary Male', *Journal of Communication and Critical Cultural Studies*, 12(2): 200–204.

Ketchum, C. (2005) 'The Essence of Cooking Shows: How the Food Network Constructs Consumer Fantasies', *Journal of Communication Inquiry*, 29(3): 217–234.

Kifleyesus, A. (2004) 'The Construction of Ethiopian National Cuisine', available at www.ethnorema.it/pdf/numero%202/ABBEBE%20KIFLEYESUS%20-%20The%20Construction%20of%20Ethiopian%20National%20Cuisine.pdf.

Kopytoff, I. (1986) 'The Cultural Biography of Things: Commoditization as a Process', in Arjun Appadurai (ed.), *The Social Life of Things: Commodities in Cultural Perspectives* (pp. 64–97), New York: Cambridge University Press.

Korsmeyer, C. (2007) 'Tastes and Pleasures', *Romantic Circle Praxis*, available at www.rc.umd.edu/praxis/gastronomy/korsmeyer/korsmeyer_essay.html.

Korsmeyer, C. (2012) 'Ethical Gourmandism', in David M. Kaplan (ed.), *The Philosophy of Food* (pp. 87–102), Los Angeles: University of California Press.

Korthals, M. (2012) 'Two Evils in Food Country: Hunger and Lack of Representation', in David M. Kaplan (ed.), *The Philosophy of Food* (pp. 103–121), Los Angeles: University of California Press.

Kotsios, P. and Mitsios, V. (2013) 'Entrepreneurship in Greece: A Way Out of the Crisis or a Dive In?' *Research in Applied Economics*, 5(1): 22–44.

Kristeva, J. (1982) *Powers of Horror: An Essay on Abjection*, New York: Columbia University Press.

Kristeva, J. (1984) *Revolution in Poetic Language*, New York: Columbia University Press.

Lacan, J. (1993 [1955–1956]) *The Psychoses: The Seminar of Jacques Lacan*, London: Routledge.

Lacan, J. (1998 [1973]) *The Four Fundamental Concepts of Psychoanalysis*, New York: W. W. Norton & Company.

Lacan, J. (2006 [1966]) 'The Mirror Stage as Formative of the Function of the I as revealed in Psychoanalytic Experience', in *Ècrits: A Selection* (pp. 75–81), New York: W. W. Norton & Company Inc.

Lahikainen, J. (2007) '"You Look Delicious": Food, Eating and Hunger in Margaret Atwood's Novels', available at https://jyx.jyu.fi/dspace/bitstream/handle/123456789/13348/9789513929381.pdf?sequence=1.

Lang, T. and Heasman, M. (2004) *Food Wars: The Global Battle for Mouths, Minds and Markets*, New York: Walker & Company.

Lasch, C. (1991 [1979]) *The Culture of Narcissism: American Life in an Age of Diminishing Expectation*, New York: Norton.

Lash, S. and Urry, J. (1994) *Economies of Signs and Spaces*, London: Sage.

Lazzarato, M. (2011) 'The Misfortunes of the "Artistic Critique" and of Cultural Employment', in Gerald Rauning, Gene Ray and Ulf Wuggenig (eds.), *Critique of Creativity: Precarity, Subjectivity and Resistance in the 'Creative Industries'* (pp. 41–56), London: Mayfly Books.

Levine, H. (2015) 'Why this Woman Made Yogurt with her Vaginal Secretions', available at http://news.health.com/2015/02/18/why-this-woman-made-yogurt-with-her-vaginal-secretions/.

Lévi-Strauss, C. (1961) *Tristes Tropiques* (trans. John Russell), New York: Criterion Books.

Lévi-Strauss, C. (1983 [1969]) *The Raw and the Cooked*, Chicago: University of Chicago Press.

Liakos, A. (n.d.) 'Historical Time and National Space in Modern Greece', available at http://srch.slav.hokudai.ac.jp/coe21/publish/no15_ses/11_liakos.pdf.

Lintott, S. (2007) 'Sublime Hunger: A Consideration of Eating Disorders Beyond Beauty', in Fritz Allhoff and Dave Monroe (eds.), *Food and Philosophy: Eat, Think and Be Merry* (pp. 58–70), Oxford: Blackwell.

Little, D. (2012) 'Assemblage Theory', available at: http://understandingsociety.blogspot.gr/2012/11/assemblage-theory.html.

Lorey, I. (2011) 'Virtuosos of Freedom: On the Implosion of Political Virtuocity and Productive Labour', in Gerald Rauning, Dene Ray and Ulf Wuggenig (eds.), *Critique of Creativity: Precarity, Subjectivity and Resistance in the 'Creative Industries'* (pp. 79–90), London: Mayfly Books.

Lorraine, T. (1999) *Irigaray and Deleuze: Experiments in Visceral Philosophy*, Ithaca, NY: Cornell University Press.

Bibliography

Lupton, D. (1996) *Food, the Body and the Self*, London: Sage.
Lyrintzis, C. (2011) 'Greek Politics in the Era of Economic Crisis: Reassessing Causes and Effects', available at http://eprints.lse.ac.uk/33826/1/GreeSE_No45.pdf.
McCole, J. J. (1993) *Walter Benjamin and the Antinomies of Tradition*, Ithaca, NY: Cornell University Press.
McGillicuddy, P. and Maze, S. (1993) 'Women Embodied and Emboldened: Dealing with Sexual Violence', in Catrina Brown and Karin Jasper (eds.), *Consuming Passions: Feminist Approaches to Weight Preoccupation and Eating Disorders* (pp. 219–234), Toronto: Second Story Press.
McQuillan, S. (2014) 'Women and Chocolate', available at www.psychologytoday.com/blog/cravings/201410/women-and-chocolate.
Malins, P. (2004) 'Machinic Assemblages: Deleuze, Guattari and an Ethico-Aesthetics of Drug Use', *Janus Head*, 7(1): 84–104, available at www.janushead.org/7-1/malins.pdf.
Malson, H., Finn, D. M., Treasure, J., Clarke, S. and Anderson, G. (2004) 'Constructing "The Eating Disorder Patient": A Discourse Analysis of Accounts of Treatment Experience', *Journal of Community and Applied Social Psychology*, 14(6): 473–489.
Marcum, A. (n.d.) 'A Visit to the Sperm Bar', available at www.prunenourry.com/spermbar/files/spermbar_nyt_theeye1.pdf.
Margaroni, M. (2004) 'The Semiotic Revolution: Lost Causes, Uncomfortable Remainders, Binding Futures', in Maria Margaroni and John Lechte (eds.), *Julia Kristeva: Live Theory* (pp. 6–33), New York: Continuum.
Mariman, J. (1990) 'The Mapuche Issue: State Decentralization and Regional Autonomy', *Topicos*, 1: 137–150.
Mariman, J. (2005) 'El Conflicto Nacionalitario y sus Perspectivas de Dessarollo en Chile', *Revista Austerra*, 2: n.p.
Martinez, J. (2014) 'Cooking with Chef Hannibal the Cannibal', *Huffington Post*, available at www.huffingtonpost.com/jose-martinez/cooking-with-chef-hanniba_b_5128791.html.
Marx, K. (1990 [1867]) *Capital: A Critique of Political Economy*, Vol. 1, trans. Ben Fowkes, London: Penguin.
May, T. (2012) *Friendship in an Age of Economics: Resisting the Forces of Neoliberalism*, New York: Lexington Books.
Mennell, S. (1996) *All Manners of Food*, Chicago: University of Illinois Press.
Mentinis, M. (2010) 'Remember Remember the 6th of December: A Rebellion or the Constitutive Moment of a Radical Morphoma?', *IJURR*, 34(1): 197–202.
Mentinis, M. (2013) 'The Entrepreneurial Ethic and the Spirit of Psychotherapy', *European Journal of Counseling and Psychotherapy*, 15(4): 361–374.
Merino, M. and Quilaqueo, D. (2004) 'Ethnic Prejudice Against the Mapuche in Chilean Society as a Reflexion of the Racist Ideology of the Spanish Conquistadors', *American Indian Culture and Research Journal*, 27(4): 105–116.

Merino, M., Quilaqueo, D. and Saiz, J. L. (2008) 'Una tipologia del Discurso de Discriminación Percibida en Mapuches de Chile', *Revista Signos*, 41(67): 277–297.

Miller, J.-A. (1991) 'Commenting on an Inexistent Seminar', addendum in Lacan, J. (2008) *The Names of the Father*, Athens: Psyhogios (in Greek, translated by Vlasis Skolidis).

Miller, J.-A. (2012) 'The Real in the 21st Century', available at http://wapol.org/en/articulos/TemplateImpresion.asp?intPublicacion=38&intEdicion=13&intIdiomaPublicacion=2&intArticulo=2493&intIdiomaArticulo=2.

Miranda, E. C. (2013) 'Neoliberalism and the Mapuche', *Senior Thesis*, available at http://digitalcommons.wou.edu/his/22/.

Monroe, D. (2007) 'Can Food Be Art? The Problem of Consumption', in Fritz Allhoff and Dave Monroe (eds.), *Food and Philosophy: Eat, Drink and Be Merry* (pp. 133–144), Malden, MA: Blackwell.

Montanari, M. (2009) *Let the Meatballs Rest and Other Stories About Food and Culture*, New York: Columbia University Press.

Moseley, R. (2000) 'Makeover Takeover on British Television', *Screen*, 41(3): 299–314.

Mouda, S. A. (2011) 'The Woman's Body and Consumer Society: A Feminist Reading of Margaret Atwood's *Edible Woman*', *IEWLE*, available at http://worldlitonline.net/the-womans.pdf.

Mylonas, Y. (2012) 'Media and the Economic Crisis of the EU: The "Culturalization" of a Structural Crisis and Bild-Zeitung's Framing of Greece', *Triple*, 10(2): 646–671.

Naccarato, P. and Lebesco, K. (2012) *Culinary Capital*, New York: Berg.

Navarro, A. (2012) 'Mensaje Presidential con Sabor a Merkèn', available at www.cooperativa.cl/.

Neocleous, M. (2003) 'The Political Economy of the Dead: Marx's Vampires', *History of Political Thought*, 24(4): 668–684, available at http://gretl.ecn.wfu.edu/~cottrell/OPE/archive/0604/att-0138/01-PoliticalEconOfTheDead.pdf.

Neocleous, M. (2005) *The Monstrous and the Dead: Burke, Marx, Fascism*, Cardiff: The University of Wales Press.

Nobus, D. (2003) 'Spectres of Fatherlessness: Social and Clinical Implications of a Modern Scourge', *Discourse of Sociological Practice*, available at http://omega.cc.umb.edu/~sociology/journal/volume5_1.htm.

Nourry, P. (2010) 'The Sperm Bar', available at www.prunenourry.com/spermbar/main.php.

Nourry, P. (2015) 'The Archaeological Dinner', available at www.prunenourry.com/en/projects/the-archeological-dinner.

Ohana, J. (2008) 'Culinary Art Therapy', available at http://culinaryarttherapy.com/defined.html.

Oliver, J. (2014) 'Become an Apprentice', available at www.jamieoliver.com/the-fifteen-apprentice-programme/home.

Oliver, J. (2015) 'Apprentice Programme', available at www.fifteen.net/apprentice-programme/.

O'Toole, M. (n.d.) 'Shakespeare's Natives: Ariel and Caliban in *The Tempest*', available at www.columbia.edu/itc/lithum/gallo/tempest.html.
Palmer, C. (1998) 'From Theory to Practice: Experiencing the Nation in Everyday Life', *Journal of Material Culture*, 3(2): 175–199.
Pamuk, O. (2005) *Istanbul: Memories and the City*, London: Faber and Faber.
Papacharalampous, A-M. (2012) 'Interview', *EGO*, 9–15 February: 24–28.
Papadopoulos, D. (2011) 'The Imaginary of Plasticity: Neural Embodiment, Epigenetics and Ecomorphs', *The Sociological Review*, 59(3): 432–454.
Parker, I. (2003) 'Psychology is so Critical only Marxism Can Save Us Now', *Paper Presented at the International Conference of Critical Psychology*, Bath, August 2003.
Parker, I. (2007) *Revolution in Psychology: Alienation to Emancipation*, London: Pluto.
Parkhurst Ferguson, P. and Zukin, S. (1998) 'The Careers of Chefs', in Ron Scapp and Brian Seitz (eds.), *Eating Culture* (pp. 92–111), Albany, NY: State University of New York Press.
Pei-Hsuan Hsieh, J. (n.d.) 'The Edible Woman: Searching for the Lost Appetite', available at http://english.fju.edu.tw/lctd/word/edible.pdf.
Peroulis, K. (2012) 'Steve Jobs and the Aestheticisation of Entrepreneurship' (in Greek), available at www.levga.gr/2012/11/blog-post_19.html.
Photenhouer, P. (2008) *Natural Harvest: A Collection of Semen Based Recipes*, CreateSpace Independent Publishing Platform.
Photenhouer, P. (2013) *Semenology: The Semen Bartender's Handbook*, CreateSpace Independent Publishing Platform.
Placenta Wise (n.d.) 'Web Page'. www.placentawise.com/.
Politis, T. (2007) 'Entrepreneurship in Greece: Main Trends & Characteristics', talk given at the London School of Economics on 13 March 2007, available at www.lse.ac.uk/europeanInstitute/research/hellenicObservatory/pdf/Seminars/politis.pdf.
Potter, L. and Westall, C. (2013) 'Neoliberal Britain's Austerity Foodscape: Home Economics, Veg Patch Capitalism and Culinary Temporality', available at www.lwbooks.co.uk/journals/newformations/pdfs/nf8081_potterwestall.pdf.
Poutzioris, P., O'Sullivan, K. and Nicolescu, L. (1997) 'The [Re]-Generation of Family-Business Entrepreneurship in the Balkans', *Family Business Review*, 10(3): 239–253.
Probyn, E. (1999) 'An Ethos with a Bite: Queer Appetites from Sex to Food', *Sexualities*, 2(4): 421–431.
Probyn, E. (2000) *Carnal Appetites: Food, Sex, Identities*, London: Routledge.
Probyn, E. (2001) 'The Anorexic Body' in Marilouise Kroker and Arthur Kroker (eds.), *Body Invaders: Panic Sex in America* (pp. 201–212), Montreal: CTheory books.
Ramphos, S. (2010) *Το Αδιανόητο Τίποτα: Φιλοκαλικά Ριζώματα του Νεοελληνικού Μηδενισμού* ('The Inconceivable Nothing: the Philocalic Rootstalks of Neo-Hellenic Nihilism'), Athens: Armos.

Bibliography 115

Ramphos, S. (2011) *Η Λογική της Παράνοιας* ('The Logic of Paranoia'), Athens: Armos.
Rasmussen, L. (2012) Talk at the TEDxAthens 2012 (YouTube video), available at www.youtube.com/watch?v=TsXkH7xVAFw.
Rauning, G., Ray, G. and Wuggenig, U. (2011) 'On the Strange Case of "Creativity" and its Troubled Resurrection', in Gerald Rauning, Gene Ray and Ulf Wuggenig (eds.), *Critique of Creativity: Precarity, Subjectivity and Resistance in the 'Creative Industries* (pp. 1–5), London: Mayfly Books.
Recalcati, M. (2007) 'Triggering Determinants in Anorexia', *Lacanian Ink*, 30: 100–115.
Red de Escuelas Líderes (2014) 'Comida Mapuche a la Sala de Clases', available at www.educarenpobreza.cl/inicio/actividades-de-la-red/actividades-zona-sur-panel/entrevista-reportaje-macrozona-sur/305-comida-mapuche-a-la-sala-de-clase.html.
Richards, P. (2007) 'Negotiating Neoliberal Multiculturalism: Mapuche Workers in the Chilean State', *Social Forces*, 85(3): 1319–1339.
Richards, P. (2010) 'On Indians and Terrorists: How the State and Local Elites Construct the Mapuche', *Journal of Latin American Studies*, 42: 59–90.
Richardson, J. (2014) 'What your Organic Market Doesn't Want you to Know: The Dark Truth about Quinoa', retrieved from www.salon.com/2014/04/24/what_your_organic_market_doesnt_want_you_to_know_the_dark_truth_about_quinoa_partner/.
Robinson, F. (2012) 'Bart: A Belgium Lightweight', available at http://blogs.wsj.com/brussels/2012/09/10/bart-a-belgian-lightweight/.
Rose, N. (1992) 'Political Power Beyond the State: Problematics of Government', *British Journal of Sociology*, 43(2):173–205.
Rose, N. (1996) 'Governing "Advanced" Liberal Democracies', in Andrew Barry, Thomas Osborne and Nikolas Rose (eds.), *Foucault and Political Reason: Liberalism, Neo-liberalism and Rationalities of Government* (pp. 37–64), London: UCL Press.
Roy, P. (2010) *Alimentary Tracts: Appetites, Aversions and the Postcolonial*, Durham, NC: Duke University Press.
Said, E. (2003) *Orientalism*, London: Penguin.
Sapoznik, K. (2010) 'When People Eat Chocolate, They Are Eating My Flesh: lavery and the Dark Side of Chocolate', available at http://activehistory.ca/2010/06/%E2%80%9Cwhen-people-eat-chocolate-they-are-eating-my-flesh%E2%80%9D-slavery-and-the-dark-side-of-chocolate/.
Sarup, M. (1993) *An Introductory Guide to Post-Structuralism and Postmodernism*, Hertfordshire: Harvester Wheatsheaf.
Schild, V. (2000) 'Neo-Liberalism's New Gendered Markets Citizens: The Civilizing Dimension of Social Programmes in Chile', *Citizenship Studies*, 4(3): 275–305.
Schurman, A. R. (1996) 'Chile's New Entrepreneurs and the "Economic Miracle": The Invisible Hand or a Hand from the State?', *Studies in Comparative International Development*, 31(2): 83–109.

Sengupta, J. (2010) 'Nation on a Platter: The Culture and Politics of Food and Cuisine in Colonial Bengal', *Modern Asian Studies*, 44(1): 81–98.
Shah-Shuja, M. (2008) *Zones of Proletarian Development*, London: OpenMute.
Sibbett, C. H. (2005) '"Betwixt and Between": Crossing Thresholds', in Diane Waller and Caryl Sibbett (eds.), *Art Therapy and Cancer Care* (pp. 12–37), Maidenhead: Open University Press.
Simon, L. (2015) 'Crime of Nature? A Woman Makes Yogurt with Bacteria from her Vagina', available at http://crimefeed.com/2015/02/cecilia-westbrook/.
Smart, B. (1994) 'Digesting the Modern Diet: Gastro-porn, Fast Food and Panic Eating', in Keith Tester (ed.), *The Flaneur* (pp. 158–180), London: Routledge.
Smith, A. (2010) 'Lifestyle Television Programmes and the Construction of the Expert Host', *European Journal of Cultural Studies*, 13(2): 191–205.
Smith, G. (2012) 'Barthes on Jamie: Myth and the TV Revolutionary', *Journal of Media Practice*, 13(1): 3.
Sotiris, P. (2010) 'Rebels with a Cause: The December 2008 Greek Youth Movement as the Condensation of Deeper Social and Political Contradictions', *IJUUR*, 34(1): 203–209.
Stadlen, M. (2013) 'Five Minutes with Hugh Fearnley-Whittingstall' (YouTube video), available at https://www.youtube.com/watch?v=qn5e5NnFQaE.
Stanford, P. (2011) 'Hugh Fearnley-Whittingstall: I Don't Eat Puppies. I've Even Spent the Summer as a Veggie', *The Telegraph*, available at www.telegraph.co.uk/foodanddrink/foodanddrinknews/8828523/Hugh-Fearnley-Whittingstall-I-dont-eat-puppies.-Ive-even-spent-the-summer-as-a-veggie.html.
Steel, T. (2014) 'Michael Pollan Gets Cooked (interview)', available at www.epicurious.com/articlesguides/chefsexperts/interviews/michael-pollan-interview-recipe.
Sweeney, W. K. (2007) 'Can a Soup Be Beautiful? The Rise of Gastronomy and the Aesthetics of Food', in Fritz Allhoff and Dave Monroe (eds.), *Food and Philosophy: Eat, Drink and Be Merry* (pp. 117–132), Malden, MA: Blackwell.
Sweeney, W. K. (2012) 'Hunger is the Best Sauce: The Aesthetic of Food', in David M. Kaplan (ed.), *The Philosophy of Food* (pp. 52–68), Los Angeles: University of California Press.
Taylor, C. (2010) 'Foucault and the Ethics of Eating', *Foucault Studies*, 9: 71–88.
The Huffington Post (2013) 'Jamie Oliver Praises Immigrants Over Young "Wet" British Workers', available at www.huffingtonpost.co.uk/2013/08/28/jamie-oliver-immigrants_n_3826951.html.
This is Chile (2011) 'A Handful of Santiago's Best Restaurants: Borago', available at www.thisischile.cl/a-handful-of-santiagos-best-restaurants-borago/?lang=en.
Tominc, A. (2014) 'Legitimising Amateur Celebrity Chefs' Advice and the Discursive Transformation of the Slovene National Culinary Identity', *European Journal of Cultural Studies*, 17(3): 316–337.

Tompkins, K. (2015) 'Sweetness and Light: A Conversation between Kyla Wazana Tompkins and Dirtysurface', *on the visceral*, available at http://onthevisceral.tumblr.com/.

Tonner, A. (2008) 'Celebrity Chefs as Brand and their Cookbooks as Marketing Communication', Paper presented at the *Academy of Marketing Conference*, Aberdeen, UK, available at http://strathprints.strath.ac.uk/15865/.

Totsikas, A. (2012) 'Interview', *EGO*, 9–15 February: 30–33.

Triliva, S. (2010) 'Women's Subjective Experiences of Food and Eating on the Island of the Mediterranean Diet', *Europe's Journal of Psychology*, 2: 170–191.

Tucker, I. (2011) 'Can Jamie Oliver Revolutionise the Nation's Schools?', *The Observer*, available at www.theguardian.com/lifeandstyle/2011/feb/13/jamie-oliver-dream-school-interview.

Turner, G. (2004) *Understanding Celebrity*, London: Sage.

Turner, V. W. (1982) *From Ritual to Theatre: The Human Seriousness of Play*, New York: Performing Arts Journal Publications.

Turner, V. W. (1995) *The Ritual Process: Structure and Anti-Structure*, New York: Aldine de Gruyter.

Tyler, I. (2009) 'Against Abjection', *Feminist Theory*, 10(1): 77–98.

Vandenack, T. (2001) 'Chile's Battleground of Culture vs. Profit', *Christian Science Monitor*, available at www.csmonitor.com/2001/0601/p7s1.html.

Vatsinas, A. (2012) 'The Crisis in Scrutiny', *Unpublished Dissertation*, Department of Psychology, University of Crete.

Veltmeyer, H., Petras, J. and Vieux, S. (1997) *Neoliberalism and Class Conflict in Latin America: A Comparative Perspective on the Political Economy of Structural Adjustment*, Basingstoke: Macmillan.

Verhaeghe, P. (2000) 'The Collapse of the Function of the Father and its Effects on Gender Roles', in Renata Salecl (ed.), *Sexuation* (pp. 131–156), Durham, NC: Duke University Press.

Via Restó (2008) 'Comida de Calidad para los que Menos Tienen', available at http://vr.tap-commerce.com/Notas/Comida-de-calidad-para-los-que-menos-tienen-135.aspx.

Vice, S. (1997) *Introducing Bakhtin*, Manchester: Manchester University Press.

Walker, S. (2010) *Cook to Bang: The Lay Cook's Guide to Getting Laid*, New York: St. Martin's Press.

Walker, S. (2015) 'Cook to Bang', available at http://cooktobang.com/.

Wallop, H. (2011) 'Jamie Oliver: British Kids are Wet', available at www.telegraph.co.uk/education/8321435/Jamie-Oliver-British-kids-are-wet.html.

Warde, A. (1994) 'Changing Vocabularies of Taste, 1967–92: Discourses about Food Preparation', *British Food Journal*, 96(9): 22–25.

Warin, M. (2011) 'Foucault's Progeny: Jamie Oliver and the Art of Governing Obesity', *Social Theory and Health*, 9(1): 24–40.

Wilson, R. (2011) 'Cocina Peruana Para El Mundo: Gastrodiplomacy, the Culinary Nation Brand, and the Context of National Cuisine in Peru', *Exchange: The Journal of Public Diplomacy*, 2(1): 13–20.

Bibliography

Winnicott, D. W. (1953) 'Transitional Objects and Transitional Phenomena: A Study of the First Not-Me Possession', *International Journal of Psychoanalysis*, 34: 89–97.

Yates, S. J. and Bakker, K. (2013) 'Debating the "Post-neoliberal Turn" in Latin America', *Progress in Human Geography*, available at http://phg.sagepub.com/content/early/2013/08/28/0309132513500372.full.pdf.

Young, J. (1999) 'Cannibalism and Bulimia: Patterns of Social Control in Late Modernity', *Theoretical Criminology*, 3(4): 387–407.

Young, M. S. and Benyshek, D. C. (2011) 'In Search of Human Placentophagy: A Cross-Cultural Survey of Human Placenta Consumption, Disposal Practices, and Cultural Beliefs', *Ecology of Food and Nutrition*, 49(6): 467–484.

Yudice, G. (2004) *The Expediency of Culture: Uses of Culture in the Global Era*, Durham, NC: Duke University Press.

Zimberg, R. (1993) 'Food, Needs and Entitlement: Women's Experience of Emotional Eating', in Catrina Brown and Karin Jasper (eds.), *Consuming Passions: Feminist Approaches to Weight Preoccupation and Eating Disorders* (pp. 137–150), Toronto: Second Story Press.

Žižek, S. (1997) 'The Big Other Doesn't Exist', *Journal of European Psychoanalysis*, available at www.lacan.com/zizekother.htm.

Žižek, S. (1999) *The Ticklish Subject: The Absent Centre of Political Ontology*, London; New York: Verso.

Žižek, S. (2007) *How to Read Lacan*, London: Granta.

Žižek, S. (2010) 'A Permanent Economic Emergency', *New Left Review*, 64: 85–95.

Index

abjection 32, 33, 35–6, 39–40, 90
aestheticisation 12, 13, 17, 20–1
Aguilera, I. 46, 53, 56
alimentary regime 12, 14, 15, 26, 66, 82–3
anorectic cannibalism 8, 101
anorectic flight 7–8, 92
anorectic person 78, 81, 88, 91
anorectic woman 7, 79–80, 83, 84, 85, 87, 91
anorexia 7–8, 78–82, 87, 88, 89, 91, 100
anthropoemic 37–8
anthropophagy 5, 37, 99
Appadurai, A. 3
appetite 7, 12
The Archaeological Dinner (Nourry, 2013) 96
artist 12, 13, 20, 21, 22
Ashley, B., Hollows, J., Jones, S. and Taylor, B. 85
A Touch of Spice (Boulmetis, 2003) 64–5, 70
'authorised Indian' 46, 48

Baines, N. 29, 36, 38, 39
Barthes, R. 3
Benjamin, W. 25, 27, 99
Benson, S. 80
Billig, M. 75
blanqueamiento ('whitening') 52
Body Bakery (Unarrom) 26
Bolivia 23, 24–5, 36
Bourdieu, P. 9, 10
Braidotti, R. 35, 81, 89, 96
Brain, J. 79

brands 10, 21, 49
Briones, C. 52
Byzantine Empire 60

cake-sculptures (de Vetten) 26–7
Canetti, E. 1
cannibal chef 29, 37
cannibalism 5, 26, 36, 37, 39, 99, 101; placentophagy 29, 32, 35, 36
Carib Indians 100–1
celebrity chefs 4–5, 9, 10, 11, 13, 29, 50
chefs 9, 10–11, 12–13, 14, 16, 17, 18
Chefs Contra el Hambre ('Chefs Against Hunger') 5, 22, 51
Chile 6, 23, 41–6, 50, 51–2; Mapuche population 6, 41–3, 44, 45–6, 48–9, 50, 51–5; merquèn 6, 42, 43, 45, 50, 55–7; renewed Chilean cuisine 42, 45, 47–8, 49–50, 53, 55
chocolate 38–9
chora 31, 32, 34–5, 48, 49, 91, 92
class struggle 68, 71, 72, 73
Cocina Chilena Renovada see Renewed Chilean Cuisine
colonialism 6, 42, 100
CONADI (National Indigenous Development Corporation) 45
cookbooks 10, 22–4, 83, 87, 94
cooking 1, 2, 11, 15–19, 22, 65–6, 86–7; self-care 21, 85
cooking programmes 3–4, 10, 17, 20, 65
Copjec, J. 90
creative adaptability 4, 11, 15, 21, 22, 31, 68

Critchley, S. 75
culinary artist *see* artist
culinary authority 9–10, 29, 31, 32, 35, 93
culinary capital 7, 10, 85
culinary culture 1, 2, 9, 10, 12, 22, 35
culinary expert 9–10, 29, 31, 32
culinary metaphorics 11, 12, 20–1, 22
cultural capital 10
cultural intermediaries 9–10

Dangerous Cooking (Tselemegos, 2010) 7, 69–71, 73–5, 89
Deleuze, G. and Guattari, F. 1–2, 14, 66, 82
developmental state 44, 45
de Vetten, A. 26–7
De Wever, B, 100

'East' 60, 61–2, 66, 68
eating disorders 80
'eating the other' 36–7
Eckermann, L. 80
The Edible Woman (Atwood, 1992) 88–9, 92–3
ego 16–17, 75
entrepreneurs 7, 13–14, 17, 40, 44, 72–3, 84–5
Epulef, A. 54–5
'European' 63
European Union (EU) 61, 66–7

FAO *see* Food and Agriculture Organization
fascism 25, 26
Fearnley-Whittingstall, H. 28, 29, 33
Featherstone, M. 20, 21
female cooking 86, 93
FIA *see* Foundation for Agricultural Development
figuration 81, 83, 89, 91, 92, 93
figure 81, 83–4
food 1–2, 3–4, 10–11, 12, 14–15, 88, 100
Food and Agriculture Organization (FAO) 22
food literature 4, 10, 11
food refusal 7–8, 80, 87, 88, 91
foodscape 2, 43

food/sex 82–3, 84, 87, 89
Foucault, M. 1, 14, 82, 83, 84
Foundation for Agricultural Development (FIA) 55–6
Fuller, S. and Hook, D. 80

gastroporn 11, 20, 21
gastrosexuality 81, 83, 85, 86, 89–90, 92, 93
gastrosexual man 7, 81, 83, 84, 85–6, 87, 92
gastrosexual regime 7, 83
genius 13–14
German romanticism 5, 13
governmentality 11, 19, 26
Greece 1, 6–7, 60–1, 62–4, 68, 71–3, 82
Greek cuisine 65–6, 67–8, 69
Greek self 61, 62, 63, 64, 65, 68
Grosz, E. 80, 90, 91
Guacolda High School 52–4
The Guardian columnist *see* Baines, N.
Guzmán, R. 47–9, 50

Hale, C. R. 46
Hannibal (NBC TV) 37, 99
Harpur, P. 2, 65, 66
Helstosky, C. 25
Hollows, J. and Jones, S. 18
Homer, S. 16, 34
hooks, b. 36
humour 75
hunger 22, 23, 24, 91

indigenous cuisine 51, 52–3
indigenous cultures 5, 28–9, 35, 45, 52
indigenous people 6, 32, 44, 46, 50, 51; *see also* Mapuche population
indio permitido see 'authorised Indian'
individualism 62, 64, 66
'insurrectionist Indian' 46, 50
intercultural culinary training 52–4
Italy 25–6

Jobs, S. 14

Kant, E. 12
Kopytoff, L. 56
Kristeva, J. 5, 34, 36, 38, 39, 91

Index

Lacan, J. 5, 15, 16, 30, 81, 88
La cucina futurista (Marinetti, 1932) 25, 26
La Ñaña 54, 55
Lasch, C. 61
Latin America 5, 22, 23–4, 35, 44, 46, 53; *see also* Chile
'Latin America and Caribbean without Hunger' 22–3
Les Toques Blanches 47, 50, 51, 52
Lévi-Strauss, C. 2, 37, 65
Little, B. 26
living labour 37, 98
Lorey, L. 21
Lorraine, T. 35
Lupton, D. 80

Mapuche population, Chile 6, 41–3, 44, 45–6, 48–9, 50, 51–5; *see also* merquèn
Margaroni, M. 34
Marx, K. 98, 99
'maternal' 31, 32, 34, 36, 39–40
May, T. 7, 81, 83–4
merquèn 6, 42, 43, 45, 50, 55–7
Mexico 36, 39
middle class 9, 21, 61, 67
Ministry of Food 5, 17–18, 19, 22
'mirror stage' 16
Morales, E. 24
Morel de Piñera, C. 23
multiculturalism 6, 44, 45, 52, 54, 57

name-of-the-chef 15, 31, 37, 85, 97
Name-of-the-Father 15, 30, 33, 81
National Indigenous Development Corporation *see* CONADI
Neocleous, M. 98
neoliberalism 5–6, 21, 40, 43–4, 84, 99
neoliberal multiculturalism 42, 43, 44–5, 46, 49, 50, 52
neoliberal symbolic order 14, 15, 31, 35
Nobus, D. 30–1
Nourry, P. 8, 96–7, 98

Oliver, J. 14, 15, 19–20, 86; *Ministry of Food* 5, 17–18, 19
Other (Eat!) 88
Ottoman Empire 60–1

Pacific Alliance 46–7
paternal authority 5, 30–1, 40, 80
Piñera, S. 45, 47
Pinochet, A. 6, 42, 43, 51
placenta 5, 28–9, 31, 32–9, 40, 91–2
placenta culinary treatment 28, 29, 31, 32–3, 35, 38
placenta reverence 5, 28–9, 32, 36, 39
Placenta Wise, US 32
placentophagy 5, 28–9, 31–4, 35, 36, 37, 38
Pollan, M. 15–16
Potter, L. and Westall, C. 43
poverty 5, 18, 23, 51
pre-modern cultures 5, 28–9, 35, 36, 37
Preservation project (Little) 26
Probyn, E. 36, 82, 87
Productos del Mar ('Products of the Sea') 23
psychopolitics 2, 4, 19, 50

quinoa 23, 24–5

Ramphos, S. 62–3, 68, 71–2
Recalcati, M. 88
Recetario Internacional del Quinua ('International Cookbook of Quinoa') 23–4
Renewed Chilean Cuisine 42, 45, 47–8, 49–50, 53, 55
resistance 80, 81, 100
rites of passage 2–3, 4, 5, 6–7, 11, 66
Rodríguez, G. 23, 47, 48, 49, 50, 51
romanticism 5, 11, 12, 13, 14, 16, 22
Roy, P. 99, 100

Said, E. 61
Sarup, M. 34
Schurman, A. R. 44, 45
self 15–16, 20, 21
self-care 21, 85
self-precarisation 21
semen 90–1, 93, 94
semiotic 3, 5, 34–6, 38, 91
sexual regime 15, 25–6, 82–3
sperm 94, 97–8
The Sperm Bar (Nourry, 2010) 97, 98
symbolic 5, 34, 35
symbolic father 30

taste 10, 12, 13
The Tempest (Shakespeare) 101
'terrorist Indian' 46, 48, 50
Tominc, A. 9
TV cooking programmes *see* cooking programmes

Unarrom, K. 26
unemployment 4, 5, 18, 19, 23

vampire metaphor 37, 98, 99
vampirism 11, 99
Vice, S. 39

Walker, B. 39
Walker, S. 87
welfare state 40
Westbrook, C. 93–4
'Western' 64, 65, 66, 68–9
white food, aestheticisation of 25, 26
Wilson, R. 49
working class 21, 22, 67, 68, 71

Young, J. 37–8

Žižek, S. 30